French Lessons

by
George East

D1125215

Cover illustration by Robin Evans

French Lessons

Published by
La Puce Publications

e-mail: info@la-puce.co.uk/georgeeast@orange.fr

website: www.la-puce.co.uk

© George East 2007

This paperback edition 2007

ISBN 10: 0952363585
ISBN 13: 978-0952363583

The author asserts the moral right to
be identified as the author of this work

Printed and bound in Great Britain by
Anthony Rowe Ltd, Chippenham, Wiltshire

Other books in the Mill of the Flea series:

Home & Dry in France
(A Year in Purgatory)

René & Me
(A Year with the Normandy Fox)

French Letters

French Flea Bites

French Cricket

French Kisses

Also by the same author:

A Year behind Bars
(The Publican's Tale)

A LA PUCE PUBLICATION
e-mail: info@la-puce.co.uk/georgeeast@orange.fr
Website: www.la-puce.co.uk

Author's Disclaimer

The locations featured in this book are all real, but some have been given false names for reasons which will become very obvious. The same applies to most of the characters and many of the situations. It is for you to decide which bits are true and which are not, though I bet you get most of them wrong.

Every man has two countries; his own and France.

Thomas Jefferson,
third President of the United States of America

Prologue

Friday, 13th September, 11.57am:

We sit as condemned prisoners, sentenced to sign away the home of our hearts. My crime has been a chronic inability to keep the financial wolf at bay, and my poor dear wife must now pay the price of my failure.

Despite our situation, it does not seem possible that when we leave this unremarkable office someone else will own the Mill of the Flea. When we bought our first home in Normandy, it was a time of excitement and anticipation. In some ways the ceremony of affirmation was like a christening. Now we are losing La Puce, it seems more as if we are attending a funeral.

Donella and I and Milly the cross-collie are arraigned in front of the local notary's desk. I am wearing the surviving jacket of an old business suit to complement my home-made Bermuda shorts and the only tie I own, and have made the effort to look my best as a gesture of respect for the passing of La Puce into other hands. The shorts were salvaged from a pair of trousers which suffered collateral damage during an attack on a bramble patch with a military defoliant said by its vendor to have been very effective on the rain forests of Vietnam. The tie was a Christmas present from a friend who thinks he has a sense of humour, and when the knot is tweaked it plays a tinny version of *Jingle Bells*. Hopefully I will not set it off during the ceremony, as that would seem like blowing a raspberry as a dear friend is laid to rest.

Alongside us are the happy couple who will shortly be the new owners of a mostly restored farmhouse, a mostly ruined mill cottage and ten acres of streams, ponds, meadowland, and - at last count this morning - two hundred and thirty eight mostly upright trees. For the keys to La Puce, the couple will be handing over a sum which would just about buy a very small terraced house in an undesirable part of town less than a hundred miles away across the Channel.

The Mill of the Flea was prized far above rubies by us, but that is its current value in rural Normandy and we desperately need the money.

When we have paid off the bank and borrowed back roughly twice as much as we originally owed, we should have enough to buy the big house further down the Normandy peninsula and set up a holiday accommodation business to help repay our new Everest of debt. As there now appear to be more Britons attempting to make a living by renting out bits of their French homes to fellow countrymen than there are British visitors to France each year, it is unlikely to be a lucrative project. But we have spent the past decade in France trying to make a living from my writing and a series of what proved to be disastrous financial adventures, so our new career path is hardly likely to be any less rewarding.

*   *   *   *   *

The long-case clock in the corner chimes the hour as Mr Remuen toys with some papers that I know he keeps on his desk purely for shuffling purposes. He then clears his throat magisterially, adjusts his trendy rimless spectacles and prepares to launch into the convoluted process of property exchange in France. It is not that there is any special significance in the chiming of the clock, and the rite was anyway due to begin over an hour ago. Like most French people I know, our *notaire* enjoys taking advantage of any opportunity for a dramatic frisson during bureaucratic transactions.

I am touched that he also seems to have dressed to suit the sombre occasion, and is wearing what for him is a restrained combination of pink shirt, yellow tie and pale blue trousers. His lime green jacket is hanging on the back of his chair. As I wait for the performance to begin, I reflect on the apparent requirement by the Fourth Republic that, along with all the other necessary qualifications, its rural representatives must also be certifiably colour blind.

After formally welcoming us, Milly, the buyers and our agent Mark Berridge, Mr Remuen begins the ceremony by solemnly reminding us of the day, month and year and why we are here. He then tells each of us who we are, where we were born, and our ages and maiden names where applicable. Although giving away the ladies' ages without demur, he stops short of revealing our horoscopes for the day, our inside leg measurements, favourite colours and the ancestry of our dog, so I suspect he has a busy day ahead.

After a suitable pause for reflection and the heightening of tension, the *maitre* moves on to the next stage. This involves the production of a large map showing where France, Normandy, the Cotentin *département* and La Puce are situated, then the display of a series of ever-more detailed plans of the location and assets of the property. I feign interest and surprise as he uses his designer pen to indicate holes in several of the dozens of hedges, fences and tree-lined boundaries, but I can sense the excitement mounting as our buyers see exactly what and how much they are getting for their money. They are a nice young couple from London, and are probably thinking that, in their part of the city, several thousand people would live in the area that Mr Remuen is casually outlining with his gold-plated *Mont Blanc*.

* * * * *

Almost an hour of signing and counter-signing has passed, and we are nearing the point of no return when the telephone rings. The years fall away and I return to the day we bought our first home in France and were sitting in a similar office. At this stage of the proceedings I was convinced something dramatic would happen to stop us getting our hands on the satisfyingly ancient and ornate keys to the front door of our dream cottage. Each time the telephone rang my heart stopped for fear the call would cause the ceremony to be aborted. Now I am hoping that the caller will be our relenting bank manager or a neighbour who believes he has a claim to some part of La Puce and wants to stop the sale. Perhaps it could even be our solicitor in England, ringing to say that a previously unknown relative has died and left us a fortune.

In fact, the caller is Mr Remuen's secretary. As he explains, it is now past noon so she is obviously concerned that some tragedy has occurred to prevent him from departing for his lunch.

Our notary reassures Madame that he has not died of exposure to my tie and shorts, replaces the phone and smiles encouragingly at the buyers as he asks for their cheque. The piece of paper is handed across the table with due ceremony by Mr Remuen. I look at it blankly for a moment then give it to my wife, who takes it as if it were a well-used sheet of toilet paper. Later, she will sew it into her brassiere for safe keeping while we cross the Channel to our British bank; for now, she puts it back on the desk and distances herself from what it stands for with one disdainful finger. For a moment I picture myself ripping the cheque up, throwing the shreds in the air and storming out of the office to reclaim our home and put up the barricades against the bailiffs. In reality, I stand, avoid my wife's eye and shake hands weakly with Mr Remuen, then our agent...and then the new owners of La Puce.

*   *   *   *   *

We gather outside the office and two small children tug at their parents' sleeves, obviously anxious to lay claim to their new adventure playground. I continue to avoid my wife's eyes, as I know that one of her greatest regrets at leaving La Puce is that our grandchildren will never swim in the grotto or climb any of the two hundred and thirty eight trees.

Another echo of a funeral service as we gather in a group, all anxious to be on our way for different reasons, yet none wanting to be seen to leave with inappropriate haste.

Mark is the first to go, and pats my shoulder as we shake hands. He knows our circumstances and feelings, and good man that he is has been an almost unwilling accomplice to the sale of La Puce.

Next, Mr Remuen moves forward to wish us well in our new home in another part of the Cotentin, and adds that he is to retire soon. La Puce will be one of his last property transactions, and he will miss us, especially after the frequency of our recent meetings. I try to make a joke about whether it will be a bad or good miss, but it does not work in French, so ask him what he plans to do with the rest of his life. He says that he has sold his town house to an English couple and has bought a cottage by the sea in the village where he was born. I say I hope that he had a good *notaire* for the property transfers, and he laughs. When I tell him this will be our last move as I think we have paid enough in taxes and fees for the pleasure of making money for him and the government, he points out that it has been a small price to pay for living in Normandy. I agree, but remind him of all the money his colleagues across France have made from people who have bought homes here after reading my books. He ripostes that, from what he has heard, most of my books seem calculated to put the English off buying a home in France. This would obviously not make me popular with the Association of Notaries, but I might just qualify for an award from those of his countrymen who have not welcomed *l'invasion*.

The stilted banter stumbling to a close, he shakes my hand again and then breaks tradition and protocol by giving Donella an awkward hug before leaving for his overdue lunch. He too knows our financial situation and understands our emotions.

We are left with the couple, who invite us back to their new home with similar awkwardness. I suspect they also know the reason we have sold our home to them.

I thank them for the invitation but say we have to leave in good time to catch the boat. They will know that the next car ferry to Portsmouth does not leave for hours, but are visibly relieved. After another round of uncomfortable hand-shaking and cheek-kissing, they load their children in the car and drive away to their new home.

We watch in silence, then my wife says she wonders how much the couple will change la Puce, and how much it will change them. She hopes they will be kind to our former home, and that it will be kind to them.

I put my arm around her shoulder and say that I am sure they will look after the old place, then remember that I have not given them the list of instructions on how to coax the best from the wood-burning stove in the mill cottage and how not to electrocute themselves when using the alleged power-shower I bought from Didier, our local dodgy dealer. I suggest we drive after them, but Donella says it would be better to go straight to our local bar and ask Franco the Fast to deliver the envelope.

She does not think I would be happy to return to La Puce so soon after saying goodbye, and besides, given the way he drives, Franco will probably arrive at our old home well before its new owners.

I agree. Franco is a delivery man for a local cider company, and a demon driver even by French standards. The last time we met he seemed unhappy, and when I asked what was wrong, he said that the PR department at the factory had recently taken the progressive step of having a *How Am I Driving?* sign fitted to the back of his secretly souped-up van. When I asked if there had been many complaints, he said the company had not received a single call, which was of course why he was so unhappy. I sympathised and said it was probably because he was going so fast that the people he cut up did not have time to take the number or see the sign, or perhaps even his van.

We cross the road to the Flaming Curtains to set Franco on his furious way while we attend the surprise party we know Coco and Chantelle are staging. It will be the fourth farewell celebration they and other old friends in the area have put on for us in less than a month, though in our present mood I fear it will be more like a wake.

But as my wife often says when bad times come, life should be an adventure and a challenge. We may have reached the end of this chapter in our lives together, but the next awaits.

PART ONE

Hark, hark the dogs do bark.
The beggars are coming to town.

13th century nursery rhyme

1

September 18th:

Dawn approaches, the page has turned and we are in our new home in Lower Normandy.

Yesterday we returned from England and the disgorging of my wife's brassiere at the bank, and have spent our first night at *Le Marais*. Although we will not sign the final papers until next week, the owners have kindly agreed to us staying here until the deed has been done and we have paid the balance of the purchase price. We have also moved all furniture, clothing and members of our menagerie on to the premises, and my old friend, mentor and sometime adversary René Ribet has been acting as house and animal sitter. As my wife said, it seemed more than a little illogical to put a fox in charge of the henhouse, but all appears to be well and there seem to be no vital furnishings, fittings or buildings missing. I am also pleased to have had such a strong link with our past to welcome us to our future.

At the moment, though, I have other thoughts on my

mind and must find a bandage.

I have a drinking friend who says he is going to write a book about all the unusual places and situations in which he has woken. His problem is finding enough time between sessions to get started on the book, and also remembering enough about the awakenings to write about them. A few moments ago, I knew how he must feel at the start of every day.

Coming to, I went through the usual process of recalling who I am, and after overcoming the disappointment, explored my surroundings. My fingertip search revealed I was lying on my back in my Superman pyjamas, with cool tiles beneath my body and a warm trickle making its way down my brow. Further exploration revealed the trickle to be blood, and worse, that it was my own.

Considering the options, my first thoughts were that I had either been taking the yearly Flaming Curtain Absinthe Challenge with the (allegedly) former French Legionnaire Thierry The Very Mad, or been attacked by Lupin, the trainee werewolf who spends daylight hours masquerading as a large and irascible ginger tomcat.

Finding my feet and the light switch, I eventually concluded that I had become a victim of nothing more deadly than an unreasonably low door frame. This would not have bothered the previous generations of owners of our new home, as being of sturdy Norman country stock they would have been close to the earth in more ways than one.

Piecing together the evidence, I concluded that during the night I had woken, groggily assumed my wife and I were still living at the Mill of the Flea and visited the bathroom without switching on the light. This will mean I have probably relieved myself in the posh bidet in our curiously toilet-free new bathroom. Or worse, in my wife's wardrobe, which is located where the bathroom door would have been in the mill cottage.

Either way, it seems I have made my mark on our new home and it has made its mark on me.

*   *   *   *   *

A little later, and I sit in the kitchen, watching the kettle and musing on the vagaries of life and fortune. I suppose that with time my surroundings may soon grow familiar and even comforting, but for the present my heart is still at La Puce. For thirteen years I have been waking in a comfortably distressed water-mill and it is strange to realise that it will never happen again. Familiarity is said to breed contempt, but not always so with familiar domestic surroundings. Except, as my wife says, when she is looking at a surviving example of my DIY skills.

I drop a spoon on the flagged floor and the noise echoes around the high-ceilinged kitchen. It seems almost uncomfortably still in this great, brooding house, and I realize I am missing the early morning sounds of the river tumbling by, the wind soughing through the missing roof tiles, and various insects competing to work their way through the remaining rafters in the mill cottage.

The coffee made, I find my way to where my wife lies sleeping. I know how unhappy she was to have to leave La Puce, but also that she will never show it for fear of making me feel even guiltier for losing our home because of my financial incompetence. This is just one of the million reasons I love her so much.

As I wait for her to wake, I think about what has happened to us in the past year, and remember a philosophical friend who believes our lives are but dreams of our own making, and that if we had the power we could awake to a better world and future. He even believes that if our wills were strong enough, we could awake and be someone else. I have often pointed out that the new reality we woke to might be worse than the dream and so, however bad things may seem, we may be better off in our individual illusory worlds. He does not agree, and I suspect because this does not suit his theory or perennial dark regard of the world and his place in it.

Somewhere in the reaches of the great marsh beyond our new home an owl hoots and is answered by at least two others. Our bantam cocks Fred and Barney react to the challenge, and I begin to feel more at home as the countryside stirs. Dawn is still some time away but our birds like to make an early start, and it is a relief to hear their arrogant cries parried from a nearby homestead. When you have cockerels in your yard, the best neighbours to have are those who also keep one. At La Puce, our closest neighbour lived more than a quarter of a mile away, but we are now part of a small hamlet and must remember that we have responsibilities to those who live close by.

For a moment I consider starting a conversation with the owls, but decide against it. I am a reasonable mimic and like to talk to wild birds, but recall the experience of a friend with a similar disposition. Moving to a new area, he set up a regular dialogue with the residents of what he thought was a nearby rookery, and it was more than a year before he found that his neighbour also fancied himself as an animal imitator and that they had been talking to each other. Their regular exchanges across an acre of meadow had also frightened away all the real birds in the area.

I look at my wife and feel a great welling of tenderness as she stirs and smiles softly in her sleep. She has stuck by me through more than thirty years of struggle, and has not wavered in her faith in my literary abilities for a single moment. I and my dreams of becoming a successful author have kept us poor, but each time I offer to stop writing and get a proper job she insists that we stay the course. When we learned that we must leave La Puce and Donella found me crying in my writing shed, she held me close and said that she would rather live in a council house than see me give up my work. I do not know what I may have done in this or previous lives to deserve such a companion, but I must be as lucky in love as we have been unlucky with money. When I was much younger and lusting for material wealth, my mother used to tell me at regular intervals that I would eventually realise - if I found those treasures - that health, happiness and the love of a good woman is much more precious than gold. I did not believe her then, and it is too late now to tell her how right she was.

My beautiful wife opens her eyes and gives me a lazy smile. I take her hand and suggest that we welcome the new day from the balcony overlooking the *marais*. To see our first dawn come up across thousands of hectares of brooding marshland should be a suitably dramatic and romantic start to our life in this enchanting part of Lower Normandy. It may also help ease my worries about how we will repay our monstrous debt to the *Banque de Voleurs*.

*   *   *   *   *

Moments remain before the new day arrives. We watch contentedly as the eastern horizon begins to glow like the skin of an English tourist in southern France during high summer. We and the rest of the world move unknowingly through space, and the aurous loom of the coming sun dulls the twinkling lights in distant Sourciéville. Our local town is a full seven miles away on the other side of the great plain where the sea once lived, and there is not a single building or road to mar the view.

A train moves silently along the edge of the marshlands on its way to Paris and work, pleasure or sadness for those who travel in it. Nearer the house, a solitary tree appears through the retreating gloom, and a low whinny and snuffle breaks the silence. It has been a dry start to autumn, so cattle and horses still graze upon the plain. But in February, we shall be looking out across a huge lake.

Behind us, the stone-slabbed roof and soaring chimneys of our new home take form, and I begin to feel more confident and even happy with what lies ahead. Le Marais will never be La Puce, but it is a spectacular property. When we first saw it I was almost frightened by its size and unaccustomed splendour, and told Donella that I thought it might be too grand. She snorted and said that was exactly why we should buy it.

Our old home was set in singularly striking surroundings, but Le Marais will be perfect for letting out rooms to people who think they think they would like to live in a place just like this. Some of the rooms are bigger than the entire mill cottage at La Puce, and even though we visited our new home half a dozen times before moving in, we are still finding parts of the property we had overlooked. Yesterday afternoon, I found a nailed-up door behind a curtain in the bathroom, and behind that a winding flight of stairs that had obviously not been trodden for years. At its end was a whole floor that previous owners had not bothered to decorate or use. If we can attract customers to our stately B &B, we shall certainly not be short of places in which to bed them down. There was also much evidence of bats and owls in residence in the loft, so my wife was delighted to have added to our retinue of non-paying guests.

The owls on the *marais* make their closing exchanges before they and the night depart, and a security lamp in the back yard of the house next door flashes on. Caught in the pool of light, a fox strolls across the flagstones, then pauses to look incuriously up at us. At my side I feel Milly bristle, and a low growl precedes a throaty bark of warning to the trespasser. I reach down and tap her muzzle lightly to remind her that we now have neighbours to consider.

Then all hell breaks loose.

The air is rent with a cacophony of yelping, baying and barking, and it is as if at least two packs of hounds have arrived to compete over which should have the pleasure of ripping the fox to shreds. Milly cowers into a corner, then we hear a distant shout and the bedlam abates almost as quickly as it erupted.

I totter to the balcony wall and look numbly into the gloom. The explosion of noise seems to have come from a large barn close by the fence marking the start of our other neighbour's land.

My wife and I stare at each other as silence returns. I shake my head like a boxer who has just received a heavy and unexpected blow, then go to find a torch.

*   *   *   *   *

I am walking along the winding track from the lane to our neighbour's house. The entrance to his property is a full quarter of a mile from our gate, but then returns towards the barn alongside our fence.

It is still dark beneath the shroud of trees, and when my torch picks out a broken-down gate, I reach out to open it. I quickly decide against this plan as the gate recoils under the impact of a shuddering blow and a pair of glowing eyes appears high above the top rail. There follows a frantic scrabbling and slobbering, and the quivering beam of light reveals what at first appears to be a very aggressive Shetland pony trying to get over the gate and at me. I take at least another pace back and then realise that the creature is not a small horse but a very large dog. Thankfully, it looks more puzzled than angry, but I decide not to come closer and discover whether it will eventually decide to ignore, welcome or eat me. From an even safer distance, I train the torch on a sign fixed to the gatepost. Below a faded photograph of the dog in a much happier mood, the notice declares that my neighbour is the proprietor of a properly registered *elevage du chien*.

Too shocked to think clearly, I pat the dog's great head absent-mindedly and return to break the news to my wife.

After more than a decade of warning readers of the

potential hazards of buying property in France and stressing the importance of location above virtually all other virtues, I appear to have bought us a house next door to an obviously thriving dog kennels.

I cannot stop the French being French.

Charles de Gaulle

2

September18th. Evening:

I believe most people who know me would agree that I am an optimist by inclination and conviction. I suspect some would say I am often optimistic to the point of insanity.

This time, though, even I can see no benefits to the situation in which we find ourselves. The dreadful dawn chorus from the barn within yards of the outbuildings we planned to convert into tranquil holiday apartments has defeated even my ability to see an opportunity where disaster appears to lie in wait.

All our plans for our new home and future seem to have been destroyed in a moment, simply because I did not make proper enquiries as to what our new neighbours do for a living.

Some years ago, I devised a list of the most important considerations for Britons when buying a property in France. It was based on the most common horror stories from people who had bought in haste and repented at long and expensive leisure. At the top of the list was a warning about the importance of checking out the temperament and occupation of your potential neighbours. This was followed by a homily about the often fatal error of borrowing lots of money to develop a large but entirely unsuitable property for holiday accommodation. Elsewhere in my books I have passed on cautionary tales about a vegetarian who bought a house next to an abattoir, and a couple who tried to set up a meditation centre alongside a nascent motorway. Now I have posted new standards in my own canon of unsuitable property purchase, and in the process broken every rule in my own books.

Another irony I find hard to appreciate in my present mood is how long we searched for and how carefully we considered our options before settling on our new home. Le Marais was by far the most impressive and beautifully restored house we had seen, perfect for our plans and a real bargain. We were also delighted to find it at the bottom of a dead-end lane and ringed by tens of thousands of hectares of national parkland which could never be blighted with new housing or roads. Now I can see why it might have seemed such a bargain buy.

Unfortunately for us and our plans for Le Marais, I did not enquire too closely about our neighbours. When I asked, we were told that the cottage on one side of Le Marais is home to an elderly widow, and that the property next door is owned by a man who likes animals. We were not told that the animals he particularly likes are dogs, and that he likes them so much that he keeps dozens in a barn within yards of the front door of the house we planned to buy.

But as usual I have only myself to blame for our predicament. We had heard the occasional yap and bark on the two visits we made to Le Marais before signing the first stage of the contract, but the absence of dogs in any home in rural Normandy would have been, if anything, abnormal. Now we have learned more about what lies beyond the fence alongside our planned development of holiday cottages, and the news is not good.

This morning I spoke to our estate agent, to the current owners, and to the *notaire* who is dealing with the exchange. According to the agency, they knew nothing of the kennels.

According to the owners, they told the agency about the kennels. According to the notary, it is normally forbidden to run a commercial kennels so close to a private home, but the premises are registered and apparently legal. Someone, he said with the verbal equivalent of the most fatalistic of Gallic shrugs, must know someone in high places. Even worse news is that the premises are licensed for the keeping, breeding and raising of up to seventy dogs.

When he had waited a moment for me to compose myself, Mr Lecroix said he will be making further investigations, and we have arranged to meet at his earliest convenience, which is next week. Before that meeting, we will be talking to a lawyer specialising in rural property and boundary law. In France, this makes him a very important and busy man, and the cost of just an hour of his time makes even the rate of our friend and septic tank specialist Albert The Very Expensive seem reasonable.

For now, I have convened a meeting on the balcony to talk about what we will do if the kennels next door prove to be a legitimate business.

All is peaceful, and the late evening sun turning the plain into a vast and rich field of gold is a cruel reminder of just how wonderful a place this could be without our neighbour and his guests.

As ever, Donella is coolly practical in her approach to our situation and how we should deal with it. She reminds me that the noise from next door is only intrusive at dawn and other feeding times. We will grow used to it, and it might not upset guests, especially if they, like us, are animal lovers. It may be that the owner is not allowed to keep his dogs so close to our home, and even if he is, we could restrict our accommodation plans to bed and breakfast guests in the main house.

I refuse to see any light at the end of the dark tunnel I have led us into, and make a couple of sarcastic suggestions. Donella dismisses my idea that we set fire to the kennels on the grounds of the danger to the inmates, and points out that my refinement of warning the owner in advance might prove incriminatory. My proposal that we specialise in holidays for obsessive dog lovers, trainee kennel maids and profoundly deaf people finds more favour, and we finally agree that we should make the best of our situation and wait until our meetings with the notary and lawyer before deciding on any drastic action.

As we look out at the big Norman sky and the distant lights of Sourciéville, my wife moves her chair closer to mine and strokes my brow as if comforting a fretful child. All that is important, she reminds me, is that we are together and well. If it makes me really unhappy to live here, we shall refuse to complete the sale. Even if we lose our deposit, we can start the search again for somewhere I will be happy. We have been in worse situations than this before and come through them. Besides, whatever the outcome, I will at least have something dramatic to write about in my next book. She is sure that my readers will find my latest cock-up entirely in keeping with the general theme of my literary work.

After thinking yet again just how lucky I am to have such a woman to steer me through the rocks that fate seems to delight in placing in the middle of our path through life, I say that even my readers will not believe that I could be so stupid as to buy a house next to a dog kennels. Looking at the moon and then exchanging meaningful glances with Milly, Donella smiles indulgently, pats my head and suggests we play a round of killer dominoes before retiring.

*   *   *   *   *

Saturday afternoon. This morning I stayed in bed until the canine chorus had erupted. I like to sleep with the windows open, but today sealed myself in the bedroom and played my favourite Iron Maiden tracks at full volume until the day was well aired. It is not that I am overly sensitive, but since we learned about the kennels next door, even a snuffle or whine

14

from across the fence makes me grit my teeth in preparation for a possible eruption. Yesterday evening, I found myself baying at the moon in frustration and misery when feeding time arrived. The philosopher August Strindberg said he hated people who kept dogs because they did not have the courage to do their own biting. I like to think that I am a dog lover, but find the barking of other people's dogs almost as annoying as the shouting of other people's children. Noise, as another more practical philosopher said, is merely sound one does not wish to hear. I understand and agree with this view, but it does not help.

*   *   *   *   *

Sunday morning, and I have avoided going barking mad for another day by persuading Donella to join me for a very early breakfast at our nearest town. It is always a delight to take part in this sacred weekly ritual for millions of French men, and it will also ensure that we will not be at home as dawn breaks.

When we were looking for a new home in the Cotentin, a prime consideration was the location and character of the nearest town. While we knew we would never find another Bricquebec or St Sauveur-le-Vicomte, we were more than happy to have discovered Sourciéville. It is an interesting town with a long history, and is also home to one of my favourite bars.

On the coast of the unfashionable side of the Lower Normandy peninsula and at the confluence of three major rivers, Sourciéville was once an important stopping-off point for barge traffic on its way to and from Paris. Nowadays, all goods and most travellers roar by on the RN13, and the canal head has become a small and determinedly untrendy marina. Many of the visiting craft are sleek and expensive-looking, but the contrasting jumble of barges, fishing smacks and other workboats in the cheaper moorings are as weathered and sturdy as their owners. The grand merchants' houses on the quayside have become civic offices or struggling hotels, and Sourciéville seems to live off itself and those who come regularly to town from the surrounding marshlands.

Like all the hundreds of small French towns I have visited, Sourciéville has its own distinctive character, yet shares a commonality with every other town of the same size. Regardless of how many retail giants stamp their footprints on the outskirts, the centres and souls of most of these solid burghs remain largely as they have been for generations.

There will be the main square which becomes a market place one day a week, and at other times a jousting centre for drivers with a score to settle. This will be a much-favoured spectator sport for those taking their ease on the benches dotted around the square, and a nose-to-nose altercation over a parking space can be more keenly followed and debated than the most hotly contested game of *pétanque*. To help with the confusion, the local authority will usually have erected no-entry signs on most (if not all) entrances to the car parking area, and each directional arrow will point towards the others. Beyond the official war zone, the square will be lined with trees and shops and creatively dented traffic bollards, and there will be an adequate supply of excellent, reasonable and unfavoured bars, butchers, bakers, florists and grocery shops. It is rumoured by some students of provincial French culture that the least popular of these enterprises are secretly subsidised by the town hall to maintain balance and the level of intellectual debate about comparative virtues and shortcomings. Certainly in my experience, the French like nothing better than a good row over who bakes the best and worst baguette in town.

Elsewhere and offstage will be those premises trading in more mundane goods and services. Now and then a naive outsider or hopelessly optimistic local will try and launch an exciting new enterprise like a wittily-named gift or book shop, but he or she will soon accept defeat and pass the premises on to the next doomed entrepreneur. So, life goes on as the outside world changes. It is small-town France that, for me, holds the key to the future of this great country. When these bastions of everyday values crumble, so will the complex yet somehow simple nature and essence of the Fourth Republic.

Although the streets are barely aired, we find the square comfortably stocked with cars. As it is a Sunday and such an early hour, a truce has obviously been declared and there are no gladiatorial contests as we pull up. I turn off the engine, then flinch as a sudden bark reminds me of our problem neighbours. I look to my right to see that a moped has pulled up alongside and is under the control of a large dog wearing the headgear of a World War II fighter pilot. The dog also appears to be smoking a cigar.

I reprise my punch-drunk boxer routine, look again and see that the dog is actually sitting contentedly in the lap of a very small man in dark clothing. The man's head is completely swathed in a black scarf, from which pokes the glowing stub of a cigarette. As we disembark and Milly and I wish the rider and his dog a good day, I ask the man about the dog, the hat and the cigar. After realising that I am a foreigner and thus not totally fluent in shrug or familiar with local tradition, he explains that his dog has an ear infection, so is wearing his master's cap to keep out the chill. The cigar is the animal's Sunday morning treat, and the dog is chewing rather than smoking it. When I ask how many cigarettes the man has smoked since leaving home, he frowns and then tells me that he is about to start on his sixth. That of course does not allow for the modest handful taken with his coffee at breakfast. I look at the brand name of his moped and estimate his average speed and the wind and general road conditions, then propose that he lives no more than four kilometres from the square. He unwinds his scarf turban, confirms my reckoning, beams and shakes my hand before disappearing in the direction of the bar. He is obviously impressed with what he must think is a foreigner's lucky guess, but cannot know that I have made a detailed study of the classic and gloriously pointless French indulgence of chain-smoking while riding a moped.

Feeling inordinately pleased with myself, I enjoy ignoring the parking meters and leaving the car unlocked (two more extremely congenial reasons for living in rural France), then lead the way across the square towards the comforting fug and fragrances of the *Bar du Bon Parle*. This is the most popular bar in Sourciéville, though not only because of the conversational opportunities suggested by its name.

In a most civilized example of French pragmatism in the acceptance and understanding of the nature of human nature, the Bon Parle is a combination of pub, tobacconist, news agency and betting shop. The owner also employs the most attractive waitresses in the region, which is another reason for its popularity. Although providing all else the average man could want, no food is served at the Bon Parle as most of the exclusively male clientele will have a wife at home. The average French countrywoman will have no objection to her mate enjoying a drink with his friends or exchanging banter with a pretty girl, but paying to eat someone else's cooking when not in her company could almost be seen as gross infidelity, and perhaps even grounds for divorce.

Of all days and times, early Sunday morning sees the provincial and rural bars in our area at their busiest and best. In the converse to the British social drinking timetable, the bars in the heart of the Cotentin are quiet on Friday and Saturday evenings. Anyone who has seen a French countryman nursing his half of beer before going home to eat and drink with the family will know why prices in bars have to be so relatively high. But on Sunday and at a time when most British pub goers are still in their or someone else's beds, the Bon Parle will be at its liveliest.

I believe that there is no finer institution than the Great British Pub, and it is the one thing I miss above all else when in our adopted homeland. But I know of no public house where I can find such an atmosphere of camaraderie and lazy relaxation as a busy small-town French bar at first light on any Sunday of the year.

For millions of French men, the routine is inviolable. Ahead lies a demanding day of domesticity and a long lunch with parents and children, so an early start is required to gear up for the day's indulgences and responsibilities. The nominal head of the household will often rise earlier than his weekday working routine demands, and arrive at his chosen bar as close as possible to opening time. On entry, he will take part in the mandatory ceremony of handshaking and verbal or physical badinage with friends and regulars. From my long years of observation, nobody can simultaneously remove his hat, shake a hand, slap a back, tweak an ear, pull a face, light a cigarette and shrug an unspoken response to a dozen enquiries as to his health as adroitly as a rural Frenchman. And all within an hour of waking and a moment of entering his favourite bar on a Sunday morning. As with car jousting, moonshine apple brandy making and moustache growing, our region of rural France naturally claims to be the champion practitioners of this weekly ritual, but I suspect every other region would say the same.

Standing back to allow our new friend to demonstrate his skills, I am impressed to see that he finds time and space to perform all his duties and still order a bowl of water for his dog, a coffee and apple brandy for himself, a copy of the local paper and a whole carton of full strength cigarettes and small pack of cigars to see he and his dog safely through the journey home.

We content ourselves with a general greeting to the bar, and prepare to drink in the inimitable atmosphere which comes free with several cups of strong black coffee, a thimble glass or two of *calva* and the bouquet of the familiar, always interesting and somehow comforting melange of garlic, French tobacco and the occasional male bodily emanation. Although I shall always be a foreigner in France, it is at times like this that I feel totally at home.

A languid hour has passed, the hell-hounds a league and more away will not have demanded their breakfast, and we are already on our third *café et calva*. Unsurprisingly, I am in a relaxed and almost contented mood. As Donella says, nothing is for ever, and as long as we have our health, our children and grandchildren and animals and a roof over our heads, we are the most privileged of people. As I say, I would rather that the roof over our heads was not within baying distance of a busy kennel complex. But with the help of the calvados and my wife's company, I am beginning to see things in a better light. When the black dog of depression visits me and I complain about our present situation and my advancing years, my wife often challenges me to imagine that I were a best-selling author with a world-wide following and a million or two pounds in the bank, but twenty years older and in poor health and all alone. She then asks if I would rather be as I am now and with what I have, or be older and richer. Invariably, I reply I would like all of the good bits and none of the bad. But I know and appreciate what she means. It is a sad aspect of the human psyche that we want what we do not have and belittle what is already ours. Somehow, I believe that all will turn out well at Le Marais. If not, we shall just have to move on and start afresh.

As I test waitress response time by gently rattling my cup in its saucer and lifting one eyebrow fractionally, I see that the boss of the Bon Parle is making his entrance. As the purveyor of so many vital services to his customers, he has high status in this community, and his relaxed yet authoritative gait confirms his importance to himself and his customers.

Mr Perruque is a small, wiry man who has seen at least seventy summers, and is clad as ever in black shoes and socks, trousers and waistcoat over a crisp white shirt. Completing our host's ensemble is a large black bow tie which sits uncomfortably around his turtle neck and bobbles alarmingly as he responds to greetings from all sides. Far more striking than the mobile tie is, however, the blackest, most patently obvious and ill-fitting wig I have ever seen.

As he has never been known to serve a customer, it seems a curiosity that he wears the traditional waiter's uniform. It is also obvious that Mr Perruque could afford a much more expensive and far more convincing hairpiece, and that he sports both the woven monstrosity and barman's outfit as a coded signal of his position and the fact that he can and will wear exactly what he likes. The terrible toupée is also perhaps a constant and blatant reminder to his customers that loss of hair is no evidence of loss of virility, or his ability to indulge his libido. For despite his age, unprepossessing looks and slight stature, Mr Perruque is the most renowned *courir de joupons* in all Sourciéville, and perhaps all Lower Normandy. He is known throughout the region as the most dedicated of skirt-chasers, and is further admired by his customers for organising his affairs so that he does not have to chase any skirts and their wearers too far.

As we wait and watch, the owner of the Bon Parle surveys the room like an elderly buzzard surveying a field of corn at harvest time, then turns and makes his way swiftly towards the beaded curtain leading to the stock room. I note that his bow tie twitches and his patent-leather footwear squeaks in protest as he sidesteps and jinks at high speed round a knot of customers. Shortly afterwards, the waitress whose attention I have been trying to attract puts down her tray, fluffs up her hair and makes her way through the curtains. The customers sitting nearby have also seen the subtle signals, and the betting commences. In many British pubs, Sunday morning is traditionally the time for the weekly raffle, with the top prize a roasting joint or bottles of wine and spirits. In the Bon Parle, the customers will be wagering how long Mr Perruque will be engaged in the stock room, and in what position and condition his bow tie and wig will be when he emerges.

Being forbidden by Donella to lay a bet on the outcome, I repeat my eyebrow gambit with the nearest waitress and catch her eye as she pauses to pass the time of day with the moped rider and his dog. The man is showing her a page from the local newspaper, and I can see that most of it is taken up by a photograph of a hunting party. It is a tableau enacted a million times a week across France, with a number of ruddy-faced men arranged in football team style. The men in the back row nurse dogs, wine glasses and guns, while those in front are kneeling and holding up their catch to the camera. All the hunters look much happier than any of the dozens of dead game birds hanging resignedly from their hands.

On closer inspection, I see what makes the picture different from so many similar sporting photographs.

In the middle of the back row, a man of late middle-age and considerable girth is smiling complacently and a little smugly at the camera. His plaid shirt is stretched across his paunch, and beneath it, his unfeasibly large penis rests on the shoulder of the man kneeling in front. The victim is obviously unaware of his burden, while all the other hunters seem to be in on the joke and enjoying it hugely. The caption below the photograph makes a witty observation about the pleasures of hunting and exposing oneself to the fresh air. To me, the picture sums up a very special aspect of French culture, and yet another good reason for living here. In Britain, I can think of no daily newspaper - however full of photographs of naked young women and breathtakingly hypocritical kiss 'n' tell stories - which would print such a photograph. Here, the moment of genial ribaldry in the heart of the countryside is seen for exactly what it is, and been chosen without hesitation to brighten the day of the readers of this family newspaper. Like peeing in public, ordinary French people see nothing offensive in any part of the human anatomy or what it is used for.

After the moped man has pointed out the key aspect of

the photograph to the waitress, he places the newspaper on the table, holds his hands apart like a fisherman demonstrating the size of the biggest fish he has allegedly caught, then nods towards his lap. She tosses her head, lets a little puff of air escape from her pursed lips, then lifts one drooping little finger in the air. Having put him in his place, she ruffles his hair affectionately, notes my eyebrow twitching and comes across to take our order.

As I am about to ask for a final round, a stir amongst the customers signals the re-emergence of Mr Perruque through the beaded curtain. A dozen wrists are lifted as the punters check the exact time of his absence, and one young man in a track suit holds up a stopwatch with a theatrical flourish.

The exact time of the brief encounter confirmed, all attention turns to the condition of the runner and rider. Apart from a slight glow to her features and badly smudged lipstick, the waitress appears unscathed. The owner of the Bon Parle, however, looks considerably worse for wear. His face is as white as his now-rumpled shirt, his bow tie is on a vertical rather than horizontal plane, and his wig has moved at least ten degrees askew of its original alignment. There is also a large crimson smear leading from the left side of his upper lip to a point just below his spectacles, the lenses of which have become misted over.

There is no round of applause, but a low rumble of triumph or disappointment from those who have placed a bet. Apparently unaware of the reaction, Mr Perruque straightens his tie and hairpiece and attends to his face and spectacles before returning through the curtain. Presumably he is going for a lie down before the next encounter, or to report to Madame that things are going nicely downstairs and all is business as usual at the Bar du Bon Parle.

Le goût, c'est la mort de l'art. (Taste is the death of art).

Edgar Degas

3

A perfect autumn day. Although the sun still glisters, there is growing evidence that we are slipping into a new season. The hours between dawn and dusk shorten as the shadows lengthen, and the keening of busy chainsaws remind us it is time to prepare for what is to come. Soon, the plain beyond our land will become a marsh and then an inland sea, and the autumn mists will imbue quite ordinary places with an air of brooding mystery. I know many people who visit Normandy say they would not like to live here as it is not warm enough in springtime, too unpredictable in the summer, too cold in winter and too wet all the year. For us, the variation is sublime, and the presages and passing of the seasons are another very good reason for making our home here.

Apart from the occasional yelp from beyond the fence and the odd thudding of distant gunfire, all is peaceful. A skein of wild geese arches high across our land, then the birds wheel in perfect symmetry to head provocatively back towards a lake and the groups of pre-season hunters who huddle aboard their incongruously small punts. I cannot think the geese will be so stupid as to fly into such obviously dangerous territory. Perhaps like me they are unable to resist taking the riskiest path; or perhaps they know that French hunters are generally such poor shots that the safest place to be is directly in their line of fire.

As I flap my arms, leap up and down and try to alert the geese with a series of warning gabbles, my wife and dog arrive on the balcony. It says something about our relationship that neither bothers to ask me what I am doing.

Cutting short my explanation, Donella tells me that we have had both a welcoming visit and a complaint from our kennel-owning neighbour and his wife. Mr and Mrs Querville, she adds, are from the Basque region of France, and seem very nice.

I do my punch-drunk boxer impression for the third time in as many days, and ask sarcastically if he came to ask me to keep the level of my musical recordings down as the noise is disturbing his dogs at feeding times. Donella says the music is not a problem, as Mrs Querville says their dogs quite like the more restrained ZZ Top tracks. They are, though, no fans of Pavarotti, especially when he hits the high C in *Nessun Dorma.*

The cause of our neighbours' concern is a series of incidents at the fence dividing our properties, and Mr Querville has requested that we try to dissuade our cat from attacking his favourite pet. I ask if Lupin has been worrying the three-legged sheep I have seen grazing by the fence, but Donella says our neighbour claims our cat has traumatised the giant dog I met at the dawn of our first morning at Le Marais.

According to the Basque Quervilles, their massive hound is actually the most gentle, sensitive and even naive of creatures, and now spends its time cowering in the farmhouse kitchen lest he encounter our cat. Their dog, he says, bears several fresh scars as a result of his meetings with Lupin, and may well need counselling before he can be persuaded to leave the house again. Although I am an animal lover, I find the news somehow satisfying, but agree with Donella that we should respond to our neighbours' invitation to visit their home and try to resolve this and any other issues. She adds that they have also suggested we bring our cat along to get to know and perhaps befriend their animals. For a moment I consider the outcome and advantages of letting Lupin loose in the kennels, but conclude that the resulting vet's bills and damage claims would certainly ruin us.

As my wife leaves to arrange our visit, the sound of a fusillade of shots followed by a chorus of oaths carries across the marshland. Taking up my binoculars, I count the wild geese as they soar over the stone roof of Le Marais and away from the frustrated hunting party. They continue their stately progress towards the setting sun, and I settle down to reflect on our circumstances and situation.

At any suitable and often completely unsuitable opportunity, it is said that the French like to use an expression which observes that the more things change, the more they stay the same. On this sunny afternoon and at this time in our lives, the apparent oxymoron rings particularly true. Although our lives have changed quite dramatically in the last month, we are still in the area and country we have learned to love, French hunters are still rotten shots, and I have once again contrived to land us in the most bizarre and potentially very costly situation.

As the English say the French say: *Plus ça change, plus c'est la meme chose...*

*   *   *   *   *

We are on our way to Sourciéville and the allegedly best and certainly most expensive restaurant in the area. The evening has long been booked for a celebration dinner to mark our arrival at Le Marais. Things have not turned out the way we planned, but we are determined to carry on as if they had until we meet with our new notary and lawyer later in the week.

Then we shall decide on our next move, which will be to go or stay.

Apart from regular visits to lorry drivers' lunchtime stopovers where the food will always be as excellent as it is cheap and unpretentiously presented, my wife and I eat out rarely. Donella does not approve of spending as much on a meal of lamb cutlets as a whole sheep would cost at market, and I don't like paying to be patronised by someone who assumes he is better than me because he knows how to fashion an unrealistic swan from a linen napkin.

Although we have had some memorable meals here, I think that eating out in France is often more about fashion and status than the food on offer. In fact, I believe the menu is often the most enjoyable offering at many French restaurants. It also seems to me that a lot of people on both sides of the Channel judge the quality of a meal by the price rather than the taste of what they pick to put in their mouths. The more astronomical the charge for serving up a sliver of liver hiding in a rich sauce, the more delicious it must be, or so the reasoning goes. Another irritation is the inverse law of cost to quantity that applies to all trendy eating places. The more one pays, the less one finds on the plate, and the less one is supposed to eat of it for fear of being seen as a *gourmand* rather than *gourmet*. This is a plainly nonsensical affectation, as, if the food were that exquisite, how could the eater not clean his or her plate? If all the people who claim to be passionate about food were truly so, they would be too fat to walk. I cannot imagine any true lover of literature being able to ration himself to just a few paragraphs of any great work each day. I have spent too many hours and far too much time looking up the nose of a waiter and down the wine list for a bottle that costs less than a top-of-the-range felling axe to join in this expensive game. Besides, with so many people in the world having not enough to eat, it seems almost obscene to elevate the simple process of cooking and eating to an elitist art form.

But I know Donella enjoys the occasional opportunity to

eat something neither she nor I have cooked, and especially not having to clear up my mess afterwards. So I will make an effort to be on my best behaviour this evening, and try very hard to ignore the cost and humbuggery.

*   *   *   *   *

We have arrived at the restaurant, and the auguries are not promising. Apart from the place having a long and silly name to do with seasons and fruits of the sea and land, the honest stone steps to the foyer are obscured by a red carpet into which the name of the restaurant has been woven. This is a very bad sign, as it will be the diners who will have to pay for this frippery. I have also seen through the window that the tablecloths are of what looks like damask, and the napkins are pretending to be water lilies. This is another depressing indicator of what lies ahead, as the material covering the table in any provincial French restaurant is a certain guide to the cost of the food put on it. And also how much we will not be getting of it for our money. This is another reason why we normally frequent eating places with paper serviettes and no table cloths.

My concerns are confirmed when we arrive at the reception desk to be confronted by a female stick insect who clearly regards herself as the star attraction. She does not actually have her name woven into the material of her flowing outfit, but is dressed as if for a night at the opera rather than showing customers to their tables. She also makes no attempt to conceal her horror when inspecting my mismatching jacket and truncated trousers. She seems particularly fascinated by my Father Christmas tie, but is clearly unimpressed when I tug the knot and demonstrate its novel audio qualities. It is no surprise when she blanches as I summon up my best French to say who we are, then takes obvious satisfaction by responding

29

in perfect English and making me pronounce my surname three times before agreeing to find it on the list. She looks even unhappier at this evidence that we have indeed booked a table and not arrived to ask if the windows need cleaning.

Eventually, she gives a deep sigh and we follow at a respectful distance as she glides in the direction of the most distant and therefore most inconspicuous tables. Perversely yet predictably the presence of a dog in such a high-class dining establishment is not questioned, and if anything, Milly receives preferential treatment as we are shown to our places.

Our reluctant hostess departs to welcome an obviously much more suitable couple, and I take stock of our surroundings as an excuse to delay looking at the menu. Although it is early in the week, most of the tables are taken, and the customers provide rich pickings for my observations.

To our left is a late-middle-aged couple who look as if they are enjoying their eating experience as much as each other's company. Both keep their eyes rigidly fixed on their plates, do not exchange a word, and appear somehow to be dining on their own. It is a trick probably perfected over their long years of marriage.

The man is wearing half-spectacles and staring intently at the small fish on his otherwise barren and ludicrously oversized plate. He wields his knife and fork like a surgeon conducting a complex operation, and removes the bones of his patient with small, precise incisions and adroit flicks of the knife. I see that he is picking up and adding each bone to a small pile which he has arranged in an intricate latticework on the side of the plate. Now and then, one of the bones falls askew and he frowns in irritation before replacing it in the desired location. At regular intervals he winces and sighs as if at some painful memory, then reaches out to his glass of wine. Picking it up, he regards the contents dolefully before drinking as if taking a dose of unpleasant medicine. To test my suspicions and pass the time, I count how many times he chews each mouthful of fish and am not surprised to find the tally matches on each occasion.

Across the table, his wife pecks at a small and lonely castle of puff pastry with nervous, bird-like movements. She is drinking more than her husband, and as she returns her glass to the table, a few drops fall upon the tablecloth. She stiffens as the man turns his head to look at her for the first time since I have been watching them. He says nothing, and regards her steadily over the top of his spectacles before shaking his head resignedly and returning to the operation. The woman senses I am watching her, and our eyes meet. I give her what I hope is an encouraging and at the same time sympathetic smile, and she responds with the merest twitch of her shoulders before looking back at her plate. I do not speak shrug, but I think I understand her gesture perfectly.

In complete contrast to this depressing epiphany, the table next to the insular pair is occupied by a young couple who would not notice if I climbed on their table and emulated in my small way the hunter in the photograph in yesterday's local paper. For them, nothing exists in the universe but each other. They are in love, and that is all they need. They treat the table between them as an obstacle rather than - like their neighbours - a defensive rampart, and arch their backs and stretch across the white desert separating them like lovebirds in separate cages. If they could, I am sure they would meld into one blissfully happy and eternal entity. The girl is achingly beautiful, with near-translucent skin and elfin features framed by short and artfully ragged black hair with a careless parting. She needs and wears no makeup, and is dressed in an open-necked shirt and jeans. On her feet she wears scuffed walking boots, but she is the most gloriously feminine woman in the room. Except, of course, for my wife, who I see is looking wistfully at the girl. I think her wistfulness is not so much because of the girl's age, beauty and happiness to be so in love, but because Donella has left her favourite boots and denim trousers at home and forced herself into a dress and high-heeled shoes to mark the occasion.

As she sees I am watching her, my wife reprimands me for

not opening my menu and for staring rudely at the other diners. I say that I am actually doing my job and observing Life for use in a future book, but she retorts that this is just a good excuse for indulging my natural nosiness while coming to conclusions which are probably totally inaccurate.

My defence is put on hold by the arrival of the stick insect to enquire if we have decided on what we want to eat. I say that we are still considering our options and she asks tartly if we are ready to order the wine. Smiling benevolently, I ask if the cellars include a large carafe of something red and cheap. This request, as I intended, has more effect on her than if I had asked if she was wearing a cheap scent. As with paper tablecloths and napkins, jugs of wine are never seen on the tables of restaurants like this.

As she simmers, I keep her waiting for a long minute while apparently studying the wine list, then order the cheapest bottle, which I note does not even warrant a description beyond year and approximate place of birth. I also note that it is more than five times the price it would be in our local convenience store.

The insect lady flits away with her shoulder blades threatening to pierce the material of her dress, and I see her pause to say a few words to a waiter while nodding dismissively in our direction.

As we go through the menu and prices and decide not to wander off the card, I hear a braying snort followed by a peal of raucous laughter, and do my best to look like a local rather than a foreigner, and especially an English foreigner.

Although I am proud to be a Briton and believe the human pantheon can and should accommodate most examples of individual character and inoffensive behaviour, I am occasionally embarrassed to see my countrymen and women letting the side down by giving other nations the idea that we are all either barbarians or clinically brain dead. Or sometimes both. The most usual offender is a mouth-breathing moron who thinks it amusing to vomit on his mates in between wrecking a succession of ferry port bars, but there are other species who would be best deprived of their passports if not their lives.

I had been so absorbed by the contrasting couples at the nearest tables that I had not spotted the group of middle-classed Britons who have apparently left their boat parked in the nearby marina. They are obviously middle-class and British because no other class or race I have encountered in my travels around the world looks and sounds remotely similar, or can do such a realistic impression of a startled horse when they think they are being amusing. It is also clear that they have arrived in the area by yacht as the men are dressed in expensive designer clothing which is designed and priced specifically to proclaim their ability to afford their hobby.

The party consists of three men of varying ages, and two women of almost identical appearance. Both wear the same sort of outfits as the stick insect lady. Both have very brown faces which contrast violently with the vermillion and purple coatings on lips and eyes. Their teeth are so white that it appears as if a great quantity of expanding polystyrene foam has been pumped down their throats and is trying to get out of their mouths. The mahogany tans have doubtless been acquired at great expense to someone, but in combination with the hugely made-up eyes and lips, the effect is to make the women look like elderly and underfed Rhesus monkeys.

The cause of the outburst of braying is one of the men, who is pouring champagne into the shoe of the woman at his side. He then attempts to drink it, but as he has no chin and the sandal is open-toed, the operation is spectacularly unsuccessful and most of the wine cascades down the front of his shirt. This brings about a renewed bout of braying, honking and snorting, in response to which the man makes an exaggerated bow and then slumps back into his seat while looking around to ensure his performance has been seen and appreciated. He is to be disappointed, as, true to Norman form, his audience has turned back to the business in hand after an initial glance. The locals have seen what they have seen and formed their own opinions, and are no longer interested. What the people at the big table do not realise is that, in France, drunkenness is generally seen as the unwelcome consequence of drinking and not the objective. The spectators will also have their views of the British ability to appreciate fine wine confirmed, as the man has just wasted at least two glasses' worth of very expensive vintage champagne.

This general lack of interest clearly does not suit the performer, who now begins to sing a sea shanty which dwells on the satisfaction of sinking French ships and drowning their crews.

As most of the people in the restaurant will not be able to understand what the man is singing, I decide to be offended on their behalf and glare across at him. He sees my look and points my wife and me out to his friends. They laugh at his remark, and it is clear they think we are local peasants having a special and unaccustomed night out. In a way, they are right, and I am glad it is so.

The noise and its maker subside, and we find a waiter carrying our bottle of wine has materialised beside our table. He has obviously been briefed by the insect lady, and clearly does not need her encouragement to regard us as the sort of people who should be washing dishes in his restaurant rather than eating from them.

In my experience, French waiters come in three distinct varieties. The best are helpful and attentive and work their magic without one being really aware of their presence. The second is the truculent type who obviously wishes he were sitting in your seat, or believes you do not know how to use a knife and fork because you are not French. The third is the most common in this sort of establishment, and obviously considers himself superior to everyone in the place, and especially the customers. This type also seems to regard each encounter with a diner as a confrontation from which there must only emerge one winner.

Our man is obviously a prime example of this category, and his manner is distinctly offhand as he pours a thimbleful of wine into a ridiculously large glass then looks around the room for an interesting diversion as he awaits my uninformed and thus irrelevant judgement. Without picking the glass up, I look at the contents and then tell him that I can see it is wine and I am sure it is in perfect temperature and condition, and that we are now ready to order. He purses his lips as I win Round One (I would have lost hands down had I obediently picked it up), then regards me with malicious anticipation. He knows that I know that he will judge my worthiness to be served by him by what I order, how I order it, and the questions I ask about our chosen dishes.

After rifling through the pages of the most expensive courses and deciding whether to take him on and blow a months' grocery budget and by so doing spoil my wife's evening, I concede and tell him we will choose from the set menu options. I will have the steak tartare, and my wife will have the fish. He sneers triumphantly as he emerges a clear winner of Round Two, then asks about our dog. I begin to explain that Milly is an extremely rare and thus very expensive pedigree Welsh truffle hound once owned by the King of Cardigan Bay, but he interrupts to explain he was enquiring as to what the dog will eat, not where it came from. Possibly, he suggests in silky tones, my obvious difficulty with French caused me to misunderstand the question.

On the ropes, I hit back by suggesting that Milly might enjoy a fillet of steak, providing it is cooked properly. The waiter stiffens and says he thinks that it would be a gross insult to the chef to ask him to sacrifice his best cuts of meat for a dog, regardless of its pedigree. It would also be an insult to all those diners (at which point he looks meaningfully at my wife) whose husbands are too mean or poor to buy them a proper meal. Fearing a technical knockout at this early stage of the contest, I settle for the suggested plate of pan-fried pet mince, provided it is left bloody and is garnished with suitable vegetables. As he will appreciate, I say as a parting shot, even British dogs know more about vegetables and how to cook them properly than most French chefs.

I watch his buttocks clench with pique as he struts away, then turn to my wife for her verdict as to the winner of the opening rounds. For some reason she seems irritated, and reminds me that I have not yet filled her glass. She also reminds me that this is supposed to be a pleasant evening out and not a silly schoolboys' playground shoving match.

*　　　*　　　*　　　*　　　*

Some time later, and we have reached the cheese course. Donella has enjoyed her trout and almonds, but my raw and puréed fillet steak with anchovies has been a disappointment. This is surprising, as I have never before been served a bad steak in France and quality is vital when your meat has not even cast its shadow on a frying pan. Milly has wolfed down her pet mince as if she were starving but refused to eat the sautéed potatoes, grilled aubergine slices and stuffed mushrooms, so I have hidden them in the ice bucket to avoid giving satisfaction to our waiter.

The doors to the kitchen now swing theatrically open and a young man heads in our direction, struggling under the weight of what looks like a full-sized surf board. As he comes nearer I see that the surface is covered with wedges of a significant percentage of the country's four hundred varieties of soft cheese. I am preparing myself for the ordeal of attempting to get through a sample of each when the youth staggers past us and towards the British yachting party.

The group is now completely surrounded by trolleys, wine coolers and side tables to support the constant flow of food and drinks they are ordering, and the stick insect lady has dedicated four of her serving staff to their needs. From her

36

perspective, the members of the group may be vulgar and English and not have a clue as to the worth and true value of what they are eating and drinking, but their final bill will make putting up with their presence more than worthwhile.

Turning away from where the surfboard is being lowered reverently on to a side table, I find that a very small plate containing two meagre slices of local cheese, three grapes and a truncated stick of celery has appeared before me. I look up and see my adversary smiling almost benignly down at me. It is as if he has undergone a complete transformation of character since we last met, and he looks like a man who has just been told a very good joke but is forbidden to pass it on. He asks if we have enjoyed our meal, and I tell him that my wife and my dog did, but I found the steak tartare a little tough and even gritty. He passes a hand over his mouth and does his best to look concerned before apologising that the chef's creation has not been up to my standards. I refuse his offer of a free piece of cheese to make up for my disappointment, pay the bill and pointedly avoid adding a tip. He seems unfazed by this deadly insult, and even helps me into my jacket before escorting us to the foyer. As we pass the entrance to the kitchen, I notice other members of the kitchen peering through the porthole in the serving doors at me, and they too seem to be enjoying a secret joke.

In the foyer, the stick insect lady wishes us a surprisingly warm goodnight, and just before the outer doors close behind us, I hear a burst of laughter from within. It does not seem to have come from the English table.

We walk across to the car, and I say how curious it was that the entire staff seemed to warm to me by the time we had finished our meal. Perhaps, I say as I open the back door and an obviously contented Milly leaps on to her seat and settles down, they thought I would leave them a big tip if they mended their manners.

My wife yawns and stretches as we pull away from the square, then remarks that perhaps the staff were more amused at the lack of ability of one of their customers to tell the difference between puréed fillet steak and common or garden pet mince.

Boy, those French. They have a different word for everything.

Comedian Steve Martin

4

Less than a week before we are due to buy or leave Le Marais, and I have not been sleeping well. Last night I dreamed that we were back at our old home, but that the giant hound of the Basque Quervilles had developed an obsessive affection for me and followed us to La Puce. I awoke to the sound of barking and found the sheets wet with what I hoped was sweat.

I look at myself disapprovingly in the bathroom mirror, then go to the kitchen and find a scribbled note from Donella by a pile of crumpled papers on the table. It says that I am impossible to live with and that she has left me.

I sit down for my punch-drunk boxer routine, then read on and learn that my wife has left me to clean up my mess while she is blackberrying on the *marais*.

Relieved that our marriage is still intact, I put the kettle on, thank Lupin for the present of a headless shrew that he has thoughtfully left on the table, then begin to sift through the mound of dog-eared notepads, newspaper cuttings, beer mats and torn-open cigarette packets which contain the essence of my next book.

It is strange to think that these mostly illegible reminders of times otherwise forgotten will one day become a hopefully lucid account of what is happening in our lives. It is even stranger to think that the book resulting from my scribbled notes may even prove popular and sweep away our financial problems. The existentialist philosopher and Gallic hero Jean-Paul Sartre was trying to understand life when he wrote a novel about a man keeping a journal in a small northern town in France. I do not suppose that the tales of our time in Normandy will ever become a publishing phenomenon, but it is good to know that my diaries of a nobody may bring some small pleasure to other people's lives when I am dust.

*   *   *   *   *

An unrewarding hour has passed and I have decided the world must wait for the next episode of our progress through life. The table top is clear, and a hundred memories and thoughts have been consigned to a green plastic bin bag, along with the shrew's corpse and the remains of last night's dinner. When we have resolved our present problems I may feel like starting work again, but for now my muse is far away and careless of my needs. Perhaps she does not know we have moved, and is still hovering above my old writing shed at La Puce. Or, more likely, over my vacant seat at the Bar Ghislaine.

I decide to put the rubbish out after I have become reconciled with my wife, and find Milly is waiting in the yard to lead me to her mistress. Before we find her, I decide to more fully explore the gardens, land and outbuildings at Le Marais, which are the best-kept of any property I have visited in France. If we do stay here, I am sure that will change.

I whistle to Milly and we set off as I wonder again at how delightful this great house and gardens are, and consequently how awful that makes the presence of a dog kennels next door.

The impressive façade of Le Marais looks over an

40

immaculately gravelled yard in which no weed would dare to show its face, and an even more kempt and -to me- depressingly formal garden runs down one side of the property, bordering the lane. Boulders are arranged with absolute precision in the middle of the lawn to form a rock garden with attitude, and a magnolia tree in full and haughty blossom guards the gate. A variety of expensive shrubs and ornamental plants are dotted around the solitary tree, and petrified hollow logs from the marsh act as planters for lines of colour-complementary perennial flowers. It is all very impressive, but a little strait-laced for my taste. I would have liked to see the odd wild flower or mole's front door offsetting the finery. If we stay at Le Marais, I am sure that the surroundings will become more comfortable.

Beyond the garden and yard is the barn we thought would make a perfect holiday cottage, and a few yards beyond that is a fence and the large and very dilapidated outbuilding housing our neighbour's paying guests. Unable to make myself enter the self-imposed exclusion zone within snuffling distance of the kennels, I turn back to walk through the stable block which runs from a corner of the house and along one side of the yard. Even the roof and walls of this long-unoccupied outbuilding have been scrupulously maintained, and is in better condition on the outside than the farmhouse at La Puce after we had restored it.

I open the door, and immediately feel that special frisson of excitement known only to those who enter any old and distressed interior and see promise rather than problems. In my experience, Britons looking for a home in France divide into two broad categories. One is made up of those sensible folk who shudder at the sight of a building which has lain unused and unloved for many years, and immediately appreciate the work, cost and emotional trauma involved in making it habitable. The other variety is blind to these practical considerations, and see only what the old farmhouse, mill or pigsty could become with the use of a little imagination, work

41

and money. Invariably, people in this category will underestimate the cost of all necessary investments of time and work and cost by a factor of at least four. Or perhaps, like me, they know the truth but refuse to accept it when standing beneath a rotting hayloft which, in their minds eye, has already become a striking if totally unsuitable minstrel gallery. As far as I know, this denial of what should be glaringly obvious is not a recognised medical condition, but it exists, and I have been a sufferer since I entered my first decomposing but irresistible French rural property. Even though I bear the scars from nearly two decades of spending small fortunes on turning animal shelters into human habitations, I still go weak at the knees when presented with the opportunity. Like a sheep attacked by a dog, I roll over and surrender to my fate without the slightest pretence to resistance.

As a long-term victim of the disease, there is the added bonus for me that the inside of this old stable block is crying out for care and attention. The main house at Le Marais has been intelligently and expensively restored throughout, and I find that almost disappointing. Although I have told Donella I am too old and weary to take on another rural ruin, the building in which I stand offers a challenge I cannot resist. Providing, that is, we decide to stay at Le Marais.

The stable block is at least fifty feet long and the walls are of irregularly sized, shaped and rudely dressed pieces of local stone. On the outside, the crevices between the stones have been skilfully pointed; on the inside, the old mortar of lime and sand has been allowed to decompose and trickle away, registering the passing of the years in the manner of an hourglass. One of my first jobs if we are to remain at Le Marais will be the interior re-pointing. This is a laborious and sometimes exquisitely painful job, as I have found the only satisfactory method is to push and smooth the mortar into the unevenly sized cracks with my bare fingertips. In spite of the pain, I find it immensely satisfying to see a wall that was built by an unknown craftsman's hands several centuries ago returned to at least a shadow of its former glory. There is also the fringe benefit that, should I decide to turn to a life of crime, I will not have to worry about leaving any incriminating fingerprints.

Above my head, the unceilinged roof space of this simple building is a cathedral of time-darkened oak. The great beams and trusses are rough-hewn and fixed with wooden dowels rather than nails, and are as solid as the day they were hauled into place. To explore such an example of how art and craft become one as I run my fingers over the scalloped marks left by an adze brings history and humanity alive for me, and is more rewarding than a tour of the grandest museum.

As I strain my neck to see into the furthest recesses of the forest of beams and muse upon the nature of time and what it would have been like to have lived when they were still trees, I go blind in one eye. I step back and wipe my face and see that I have not been a victim of an Act of God, but of a careless or malicious bird. The sound of frantic fluttering is followed by another salvo of ancient dust and droppings, and I retreat to the doorway as at least a dozen pigeons take off and wheel around the roof space. After further spattering the walls and floors, their flight leader finds a missing tile in the roof, and they are gone.

I wipe my face again and see that Milly has not joined me in the stable block. She is sitting in the yard, framed by the open door, and when I call her to come in and see the promise of the old building she averts her eyes and lies down. This is curious, as like all collies, Milly is an inquisitive and companionable dog, and it is not like her to miss the chance of exploring new territory. I shrug and close the door and ask her to take me to Donella. When I reach down to stroke her head, I see that she is trembling. It is not possible that my dog would be fearful of a flock of pigeons, but something about the old stable block has clearly spooked her.

*   *   *   *   *

43

On our way to where my wife will be harvesting enough blackberries to get us through a lifetime of fruitless winters, we stop off to see how our chickens are settling into their new home.

Although she would not admit it, I believe a prime consideration for Donella when choosing Le Marais as our new home was the size and splendour of what has become the chicken run and coop, and it is almost as luxurious and well-appointed as the human accommodation.

Like many Norman countrymen, Georges enjoys keeping and caring for some species of birds as much as he relishes killing others, and the *pigeonnier* at Le Marais is a very grand affair. Leading on from and adjoining the stable block, it is an ornate two-storeyed building with a roomy and expensively tiled ground floor. The keeper's entrance is a heavy studded door which would not look out of place beyond the portcullis of a very small castle. Above the living quarters is a dome punctuated by a number of what look like miniature dormer windows, through which the residents can come and go freely without the risk of an encounter with any earthbound predator. The most agile or determined fox would be unable to mount the curved surface, and our two cockerels and their spouses are clearly as pleased with their new home as is my wife. The former occupiers of this pigeon palace have been moved along with the rest of Georges' livestock to his fields and outbuildings across the track, but the birds I encountered in the stable block obviously resent being dispossessed of their stately home.

Turning the corner, I see that Fred and Barney the bantam cocks are preening and parading in the small courtyard leading to their new home, while the dispossessed occupants coo their displeasure from the branches of a nearby plane tree. Our hens Gert and Daisy are ambling companionably around the garden behind the stable block, and all is obviously well in their small world.

While I settle down on a feed bin to roll a cigarette and

pass the time of day with our chickens, I notice that Milly has trotted over to the boundary fence. Despite my warning call, she pushes her muzzle through the wire netting, and then gives a small but obviously enticing snuffle. There is a movement by the door of our neighbour's farmhouse, and a huge form comes lolloping towards the fence. Like even the most apparently sensible of male humans, the craven devil-dog from next door has allowed the allure of the opposite gender to overcome all caution. His rashness is punished almost immediately as a grey streak flashes across the courtyard and lands halfway up the fence, talons flailing. The great black hound lets out a despairing wail and retreats to the farmhouse with another souvenir of our cat's ferocity, while Lupin returns to his observation post to lick his bloodied paws with obvious relish. The inevitable result of the encounter is that every dog in the barn alongside the fence gives voice, and I am reminded again of the downside of living next door to a thriving canine boarding house.

*　　　*　　　*　　　*　　　*

Although she is almost a mile from the house, we have tracked my wife down by following a trail of denuded bramble patches.

We both find picking blackberries almost as difficult to resist as stopping picking them, and Donella has clearly given in to the compulsion to take maximum advantage of a spectacularly bounteous crop.

With the wettest August on record and some brief but very sunny spells at exactly the right time, it has been a bumper year for all wild fruits, and I have never seen such luscious blackberries in such profusion. If they would help any species of wildlife survive through the winter months, my wife would of course not take a single berry. But she knows that in a week they will fall and rot and so have lived in vain. The

45

thought of such waste offends her, so the next month will be devoted to an orgy of preserving the essence of summer. I will then have the duty of spreading my toast thick with blackberry jelly, and anointing my cheese, meat and anything else even vaguely suitable with apple, blackberry and chilli chutney. Every spare bottle and jar and less suitable container will be pressed into service, and shelves will groan with their temporary burden of blackberry cakes, pies and crumbles. In years to come, we will be toasting the fruits of a summer long gone with glasses of blackberry wine and port, and even our closest friends will stop calling for fear of being overwhelmed with gifts of sweet richness in unusual form. If there is anything useful which can be done to or with a blackberry before it falls from the stalk, my wife will do it. I am pleased to see her in such a creative and happy mood at this time of year, but even I can become jaded with the singular flavour of blackberry soup, tea and even toffee.

*   *   *   *   *

We have hobbled back to the house under the burden of three log baskets filled to the brim. After a fruitless attempt to rid my hands of the stain, I have retired to my new writing shed to see what is happening elsewhere in France and beyond.

Each year, hundreds of readers send e-mail messages to say how much they like or dislike my books, and many have become distant friends. It intrigues me to learn about so many different lives and places, and to broaden my mind and knowledge a little without the necessity of travel. I am also privileged to encounter so many such diverse attitudes, ambitions and philosophies. I shall probably never meet a fraction of these intimate strangers, and perhaps it is better this way. Some of the handful of my e-correspondents I have met did not fit remotely in with my perception of what they would be like in the flesh, and I obviously disappointed most of them.

I press the necessary buttons, and am soon continuing my debate with a professor at a university in Rheims. Recent subjects include the comparative strengths and weaknesses of Kant, Jung and Descartes, and whether the plural of Cornish pasty should be pasties or pastys. Another crucial issue we feel we must resolve before we die is if the plural of ox is oxen, why are more than one fox not called foxen? I recommend my correspondent to a farmer friend in Padstow for a definitive ruling on the pasty question, and move across the Atlantic to reply to a former London policewoman who now lives in California. She also owns a cottage in Brittany, and is counting down the days until she and her husband are free to move there. 1,987 days must pass before they start their new life, and her husband has been working on a list of all the good reasons for living the rest of their lives in rural France. So far, he has written down more than a hundred, but they are both aware that any adventure carries a risk. As she says, they are burning their bridges and it is quite possible that they might be disappointed with living full time in a place where they had previously only spent holidays. But if they don't try it, they will never know. I agree with her and observe that most of us know that we will not like the result of jumping off a high building, but in many other matters one sometimes has to suck it and see.

The next message is from a new contact with a confession to make. She believes that she may be the only person in France to have employed a one-armed bricklayer. The lady goes on to explain that she had need of some urgent renovation work to her crumbling cottage in the Dordogne, and met what we are now supposed to call the differently-abled craftsman in a local bar. Due, as she says, to a combination of strong drink and inattention, she did not notice the man's disability during their meeting. It was only when he turned up to start work and took off his false arm with his jacket that she realised it was going to be an interesting working relationship. The system they have evolved is for her to hold the brick while

47

he butters it with mortar then directs her where to place it. Far from being put out by the arrangement, my new friend says that there are two specific advantages. One is that she feels she is taking an active part in the restoration of her beloved cottage; the other is that her employee is the fairest of men, and only charging her half the going rate for a more fully-equipped craftsman.

I like Frenchmen very much, because even when they insult you they do it so nicely.

Cabaret singer and femme fatale Josephine Baker

5

Four days before we must make up our minds to stay or go. The canine dawn chorus reached new levels of beastliness this morning, so I sent Donella to complain. She came back with a newborn spaniel in her arms and reported that a happy event had occurred during the night, making Mrs Querville late with breakfast for her lodgers. It was all I could do to persuade my wife to take the dog back.

This afternoon we are meeting with the lawyer who specialises in the legal intricacies of property deals. But before being persuaded into my formal clothes for the third time in less than a fortnight, I have been despatched to put the rubbish out.

While ferrying the bags to the gate, I hear an unfamiliar sound and see a car coming down the lane. As the country roads and even lanes of rural France become ever busier, it is another attraction of Le Marais that in the five days we have been here I have seen more foxes and pheasants passing our house than motor vehicles.

I put the last bag on the pile by the gatepost and look up to see that the car is being driven by the person who still owns the house in which we are living. Georges pulls up at the corrugated-iron barn opposite, and we both find a distraction to excuse ourselves from looking in each other's direction. Ours will be an awkward meeting, as he now knows that I know about the kennels next door.

My landlord gets out of the car and stands by the bonnet as he selects the key to the padlock on the door of the giant tin shed. I occupy myself with re-tying the neck of a rubbish bag which was already adequately secured, then decide I can put off the moment of acknowledgement no longer. He has obviously had the same thought, and I look up to see him watching me. I straighten and wish him a neutral good morning, and he responds in the same manner. We both stand regarding each other awkwardly, then he turns towards the door of his barn as I find something interesting about the hinge on his gatepost.

When Georges first took me around his land and lakes and outbuildings on the other side of the lane, he said he would be converting the roadside barn into a meeting place and bar for his friends and fellow hunters. Although I was not born in the village and am thus ineligible as a member of the official hunting association, I would always be welcome in the clubhouse. At the time, we joked about naming it The Two Georges, and about the convenience of my having a local so close to my new home. Now he has claimed he told the agency about the kennels next door and knows they have told me they had no knowledge of the business, things have changed. Georges will probably also know that I have spoken to Mr Lecroix about withdrawing from the exchange, and we will be technically squatting in his home if this happens. Whatever the outcome of our meeting with the property lawyer and the notary tomorrow, I cannot see how my friendly relationship with the present owner of Le Marais can be restored.

The sound of another engine interrupts my thoughts, and I see a column of smoke approaching from the direction of the marshlands. The vertical cloud arrives and begins to disperse on the afternoon breeze as the clanking, grinding noise falters and dies. I then realise I have been privileged with what elsewhere would be a very rare sighting.

Rural France is rich territory for those interested in the history and usage of agricultural machinery during the past two centuries, and revealed by the clearing of the smoke is a tractor that would have been going about its business before I was born. Over our years in Normandy I have become something of an amateur authority on all aspects of this fascinating work vehicle, and have driven, raced and helped repair them. I am probably one of the few non-Norman country people who would know how to start a reluctant tractor on a frosty morning with a tot of bootleg apple brandy or a squirt from a deodorant spray can. The latter being not nearly so common in the Cotentin countryside as the former, the calva kick-start is usually the preferred method. I am also proud to be an honorary member of the North Cotentin Tractor Collective, which unsurprisingly claims the most diverse and complete collection of vintage tractors of any similar society in Europe, if not the world. A singular distinction of our association is that the tractors are in daily use. But in all my years in the region, I have never seen a farm vehicle of this age still working for its living. Unless I am mistaken, it is an original 1935 'die-hard' Farmall F-20, probably abandoned in the area by the American forces after D-Day as already being too old to bother taking home with them.

As the driver enjoys a coughing fit before climbing down from the distinctive bucket seat, I see he is a stocky man of middle age, and wearing what looks ominously like an official peaked hat. I look closer and note that there is a brass badge pinned to the breast pocket of his jacket. This is even more worrying, as it signifies that the wearer is an employee of the commune.

Beneath and fortuitously supporting his oversized hat, the man's ears are so prominent that their drag factor must surely

51

deduct at least five miles an hour from the cruising speed of his tractor, while his complexion reminds me of an overdressed salami and tomato pizza. His giant hand-rolled cigarette is making almost as much smoke as his tractor, and one of his eyes is regarding me in a distinctly unfriendly manner. I follow the general direction of the other eye, and see it is fixed accusingly on my collection of assorted bin liners, sacks and boxes. More smoke drifts away across the *marais*, and I see that the tractor is attached to a trailer which contains several rows of colour-coded plastic bins. It does not take me long to deduce that my visitor is the commune refuse collector. This would also explain the official hat and his special interest in my rubbish, and why he is obviously not happy with what he sees.

Although we have been at Le Marais for less than a week, the pile by the gatepost is so mountainous because we brought all but two of the dozens of sacks from La Puce. Leaving our old home free of rubbish was more than the common courtesy it would have been in England. Knowing what we know, we did not want the new owners to start on the wrong foot with the refuse inspectorate of Néhou.

From a foreign viewpoint, it is another bemusing contradiction of our adopted country that a society can be so easy-going about so many other aspects of public life, yet so pernickety about apparently trivial matters. All across rural France, men pee in public and drive unlicensed cars that would be refused entry to any self-respecting junkyard in Britain. People feel free to smoke in officially forbidden areas and ignore many unpopular laws and regulations without fear of prosecution or disfavour. But to transgress the local waste disposal canons is to risk public censure and an official reprimand or fine. I have not heard of anyone being sent to prison for refusing to conform to the local rubbish rules, but I do not wish to become the first foreign martyr.

Every community has its own arrangements for refuse collection, and the arrangements vary from commune to commune. After the Euro-edict banning the traditional method of dumping one's household waste (or anything else you did not want) in a hole on the outskirts of the village, inevitable disputes arose concerning how best to deal with the new laws. Smaller, isolated communities like this one made their own modest arrangements, while some of the larger villages got together to share the cost of buying and running a proper dustcart. This may seem a sensible idea in principle, but proved not so in practice. Endless meetings were held on neutral territory to decide which type, brand, size and cost of vehicle should be chosen, and the most efficient and cost-effective methods of manning and using the vehicles. Most contentious of all was the issue of the best routes for the weekly collection, with social status often taking precedence over geographical logic. There was also the problem of exactly what should constitute household rubbish, and how to make full use of the expensive vehicles. Being Normans, all the villages and their residents naturally wanted to get their money's worth, and bitter disputes were sure to ensue. Some communities were accused by others of using the dustcart as a taxi service to and from market or for special group gatherings like weddings and funerals, and one farmer in our area threatened to stop paying his rates when the bin men refused to take away a dead cow he had left on the verge with his weekly rubbish.

Experienced in the general attitude to refuse collection and disposal in the French countryside, I should have kept my excess baggage in the outbuildings until we are granted access to the local rubbish tip, but gaining permission or even finding it could take months.

I know that the mayor of Nulleplace is a stickler for the rules he has invented, and that access to the village *déchetterie* is even more rigidly controlled than entry to a particularly secretive Freemasons' lodge. This is not unusual in rural France. Amongst the official documents awaiting us on arrival at Le Marais was a lengthy form to be completed and presented at the mayoral office together with three items of formal identification. With the form was a diagram of the layout of the tip, detailing the location of the six rubbish skips and what may or must not be put in them. There was also a notification of opening times, which do not include weekends, Wednesday afternoons and alternate Thursday and Fridays, public holidays and, naturally, the sacred two hours from noon. On the production of the (correctly) filled-in form and *bona fide* identification, the accompanying letter explained, we would be granted a resident's permit of access. This would be forwarded to us in due time, personally signed by the mayor and complete with the passport-style photograph we must provide on application. At that time, we would also be told where the tip was located. No mention was made of DNA scanning or retina eye-testing to confirm the identity of would-be users, but only, I suspect, because that level of technology has not as yet reached the rubbish tips of rural France.

I had hoped that the extra bags might be taken without a fuss if I left them at the gate and the roundsman thought the house unoccupied, but with the arrival of the official collector, I have been caught red-handed. Worse, I now run the risk of being exposed as trying to palm off rubbish which I created while living in another community.

This would not be a good start to our life here, so I attempt to distract the driver by introducing myself and complimenting him on his tractor. While clearly impressed by my knowledge of the vehicle's manufacture, specification and origins, my visitor's left eye stays focused on the bags, and when I ask if I can help by putting the bags on the trailer he looks at me as if I had asked if he would like to dance.

After sniffing the air suspiciously, the man produces an identity card which proclaims him to be Albert Poubelle, *gardien generale* of the marshlands. At first I think that this is an apt and amusing sobriquet rather than a family name, much in the way that small Welsh communities would have their Jones the Milk or Evans the School. In the Cotentin as in rural Wales, tradition and intermarriage in small communities can otherwise lead to confusion. Then I realise it is hardly likely that this man or his mayor would make jokes about such a serious matter of waste collection and disposal. Unlikely as it seems, the local refuse disposal overlord really is called Mr Dustbin.

Then I recall that familiar objects are often named for their inventors, and ask my visitor if he is by chance related to the famous Monsieur Poubelle. The man's ears twitch and the errant eye swivels to focus on me, and I realise my hunch has paid off. He nods, tries to look unassuming while sucking on his cigarette and regarding it and me at the same time, then says he is, in fact, a direct descendant of the great Eugene Poubelle. As history records, I am reminded, Mr Poubelle was born in Normandy, became Prefect of the Seine and in 1884 was the first official in all France to decree that rubbish in his area should be regularly stored and collected in containers. Thus, his name is spoken millions of times each day throughout the country, and a wreath is laid on his grave in the Aude region every year by environmental groups.

I concentrate on the less wayward of the guardian's eyes and make appropriate expressions of interest and encouragement as he gives me a detailed account of the career paths of every male descendant of the original Mr Poubelle. All, I learn, have remained faithful to the family tradition of the eldest son going into waste disposal. As my interlocutor reaches the present day and his own career highlights, I sidle towards the pile of bags with the intention of slipping them on the trailer unnoticed.

Unfortunately, it seems that my ruse has backfired, and rather than distracting him from the business in hand, Albert Poubelle's peroration has obviously made him even more aware of his responsibilities.

Scenting the air again, he says gravely that he has reason to believe that my bags have not been correctly sorted, and he is unable to take them until this has been done and verified. As I have shown such an interest in his family history and an obvious enthusiast for vintage tractors, however, he will help me with the task.

*   *   *   *   *

Our rubbish mountain has disappeared, and I am waving as Albert and his tractor disappear into the gathering dusk and an all-enveloping shroud of engine smoke. I have found that there is nothing like sharing a dirty job to forge a friendship, especially if the work is followed by a drink or two. I have also made further progress with my studies regarding French attitudes to uniforms and (even more so) the Official Hat, and how the doffing or donning of either can completely change the character of its owner. This is particularly true of policemen and sometimes even applies to traffic wardens, but excludes priests and all chefs, especially when they are interrupted at a critical moment in their work.

When Albert was persuaded to come into the house for a whisky break, he removed his hat and became another person. I have seen this instant metamorphosis from petty bureaucrat to affable accomplice too often to believe it a coincidence. With his hat on, Albert is a severe and implacable guardian of all rules, procedures and regulations concerning the commune. With his hat off, he is only too happy to advise on how to get round them. This peculiarity is also a perfect example of the ambivalent attitude of the French towards all matters bureaucratic.

When we returned to our work, I noticed that Albert had tucked his hat into his jacket pocket. As I began to sort through one of the remaining bags, he stayed my hand, picked the sack up and threw it with almost cavalier abandon into the trailer. The others quickly followed, and he looked at me with both eyes and shook my hand warmly before climbing on to the tractor. He knew that I knew how much this effort of deliberate dereliction of duty had cost him.

It is such small incidents that I believe define a race, and

56

another good reason why my wife and I so enjoy living in this beguiling land.

*   *   *   *   *

We sit in another unremarkable office with an interesting clock, and I hope we will not be expected to pay for every second ticking away as we await the arrival of our high-powered *avocat*. As in Britain, the higher the fee the professional classes charge for their services, the more relaxed they seem about keeping their customers waiting; naturally, the more grateful one is supposed to be for the audience when it finally takes place.

To pass the time, I have been eavesdropping on the telephone conversations of the lady guarding the door to where Mr Couteuse is presumably busy unbending paper clips until he has kept us waiting long enough to demonstrate his business, importance and thus justify his charges. So far, I have learned a little about the problems of a farmer in Calvados who believes a neighbour is stealing his land by the wheelbarrowful. I have also learned a lot about the lady's current affair with the owner of the funeral parlour across the road. It is not that the woman believes that as a foreigner I will not understand what she is telling her friend about their dalliances on and even in hopefully empty coffins. It is just that she is French and does not mind me knowing.

Although I am worried about how much we are paying to receive the inside information on the comfort ratings of various caskets, I am almost disappointed when the door behind us bursts open as the lady reaches the climax of her tale. I look over my shoulder, and see a man who appears to have his head on upside down. Closer inspection reveals that he is completely bald and wearing a very full and luxuriantly-coiffed beard. He is also moving very fast. As the human whirlwind passes the

57

desk, the momentary vacuum his passage creates causes a pile of papers to be sucked from the desk. They hang in the air for a second, then the man is gone, the door slams and the papers flutter to the floor. Unmoved, the receptionist finishes her conversation, then collects the papers from the floor and tells us that Maitre Couteuse awaits our pleasure.

*   *   *   *   *

If we are to pay for our legal consultation on a time basis, we have certainly had our money's worth. Mr Couteuse speaks as fast as he walks and smokes, and our meeting lasted for little more than fifteen minutes and three cigarettes.

It is said that a good barrister never asks a question in court to which he does not already know the answer. Going by our encounter, Mr Couteuse must be at the top of his professional tree. He did not ask us a single question, and as well as having a very fast mind he may also be a telepath. Each time I opened my mouth to ask about a point of law or a possible solution, he answered my as-yet unspoken query. Glancing occasionally at a sheet of notes provided by the notary, he paraphrased the relevant laws and the likely outcome of any legal action, and concluded with our options.

Our situation is now clear, and even worse than I had thought.

Although even in France it is illegal to run a kennels so close to a dwelling place, our neighbour has been given special dispensation. The reason for this exemption is not clear, but the Quervilles have every right to keep up to seventy dogs in the barn next to our fence. We could query and challenge the granting of the licence, but it is alleged locally that a close relative of Mr Querville works in the administrative headquarters for this region of France. She is also alleged to be very close to her boss, and if this is true our advocate thinks that any efforts to get Mr Querville's licence revoked would be a waste of time.

Even more of a shock was the news that we are already committed by law to buying Le Marais.

The *Acte Finale*, Mr Couteuse explained, is merely the conclusion of a process to which we were irrevocably compromised when we signed the *compromise de vente*. As we would or should know, escape clauses in the form of special conditions could have been inserted in that document. We did, he noted, put in a proviso that we would not complete the transaction if the sale to La Puce had fallen through. We could also have stipulated that a rainbow must appear in the sky on signing day and have our deposit returned if it did not. Unfortunately, we did not think to make a condition that we would not buy Le Marais if there was a busy canine lodging and breeding centre next door. There is a faint hope that our notary may be persuaded that, in his opinion, the sale is unsound and should not go through. But that, our specialist thinks, is unlikely.

Having explained our situation in law, Mr Couteuse turned to our options. We could fight the case on the grounds that it was unreasonable to expect anyone to buy a home so close to a likely source of unacceptable noise, but this would require us to prove that we did not know about the kennels. To do this, we would have to persuade a French court that either a French estate agency or the French owners of Le Marais deliberately withheld the facts about our neighbour's business from us, the foreign buyers. Although those who sit in judgment in French courts are as impartial and unbiased as could possibly be imagined, he would leave it to us to think about the odds on a decision in our favour. If we did wish to go ahead and press our suit, he warned us that the case could go on for years, and could cost more in legal fees alone than the property was worth.

As to our other options, it seemed to him we have just two. We must either complete the transaction and learn to live with our neighbours and their dogs, or forsake our deposit and simply leave Le Marais and France. Our home country is in the European Union, so we could be pursued and made to complete the deal. But, in his opinion, the courts would be unlikely to do so for such a relatively small amount of money. As Mr Couteuse said they like to say in French legal circles when this sort of situation arises, there is a lot of water in the English Channel.

*   *   *   *   *

We are taking coffee in the square of the region's main town. At the same time, we are trying to take in the significance of what Mr Couteuse has said.

Apart from two ancient and quite spectacular places of worship, we do not find St Lo an especially characterful place. It is a bustling and prosperous town, but many of the original buildings and shops were flattened during the D-Day engagements. This example of collateral damage from so-called friendly fire also explains why German visitors are often more welcome than American tourists. It is not that the Normans are ungrateful for the relief of their homeland, but that the carpet-bombing and bombardments in some areas killed more civilians than the occupying forces ever did.

I glare at a waiter in a trendy long white apron who is obviously waiting for us to leave so he can serve some proper customers, and then reprise our situation. Now we have met the property law specialist, it seems our only hope is that our notary will find the sale of Le Marais unsound, so cancel it and give us our money back. If not, we must stay on and change our plans for creating a holiday centre within yards of the kennels. Or we could do a moonlight flit. Ironically, leaving the place in which one is living without telling anyone is normally a ruse to avoid paying the rent. In our case, it would cost us tens of thousands of pounds.

Donella is made of sterner stuff and is keen to stay at Le Marais, but I am not so sure. If every bark reminds me of what a mess I have made of our move from La Puce, I think I would rather just run away.

*   *   *   *   *

I have taken a detour on our way back to what may be our very temporary home, and suggested we stop for a drink in the first unfamiliar bar we see. Though a keen collector of unusual and out-of-the-way bars, this part of the peninsula is unfamiliar so I am hoping to add to my list of unique oases. Although I have not told Donella, I have also been looking out for *A Louer* signs on any isolated and unoccupied cottages we pass. If we are to leave Le Marais with Mr Lecroix's blessings, we shall need a temporary home while we look for our next permanent one. If he does not agree to cancel the sale, we may need a hiding place until we can make our arrangements to flee the country.

Passing through a hamlet on the back road to our local village of Nulleplace, I am surprised to see that the old grocery store and bar has been re-opened. The property and licence were on sale when we first looked for a new home in the area, but even I did not see how it could have a future. Besides, Donella would not have allowed me to buy and run it at any price.

Like so many similar rural enterprises, the *bar-épicerie* at Nulleplace will have fallen victim to changing habits and the arrival of yet another supermarket in the area. The majority of food items on sale in Super-U are priced at less than the previous owner of the little store could have bought them, and the closure would normally have meant another loss to the traditional fabric of the countryside. But it appears that someone has decided he can make a bar work here again. As

61

only a madman or an innocent abroad would open a pub in a hamlet that is small even by French standards, I am not surprised to see a flag of St George hanging limply alongside the tricolor above the door.

The name of the establishment is further evidence of foreign ownership, as it is called *Le Entente Cordiale.* This declaration of the new owner's amicable intentions may be well meaning, but is unlikely to have the intended impression on the locals. In France, it is not only pedants who become inflamed by the omission of a single apostrophe and addition of a surplus letter. Also, as no French sign writer would have committed such a crime, the resulting vowel clash is a permanent reminder that alien rather than local craftsmanship has been used for the job.

Parking our car next to a monstrous motorcycle of the sort that only born-again British bikers of a certain age can afford, I see that a sandwich board beside the entrance confirms the proprietor's desire to offer the best of both cultural worlds. On one side is a list of traditional French bar snacks, while the other boasts a selection of typical English pub grub. The 'Best of British' dishes include Chicken Tikka, Spaghetti Bolognese, Moussaka and Chili-con-carne. Obviously undecided as to which nation is entitled to lay claim to another house speciality, French Toast has been added to the bottom of each list. On the British side, however, the same delicacy is offered with optional Marmite and/or Cheddar cheese.

Although intrigued by what we may find inside, we sit and watch for a moment as an old and obviously retired hunting dog emerges from the back yard of a cottage opposite the bar. It crosses the road, pauses by the doorway and sniffs suspiciously, then contemplates the menu. After a moment it shuffles forward, cocks a leg and pees on the sandwich board. The chalk writing blurs and runs, and I note that the dog has chosen to relieve himself on the British side of the board. Although his choice of target was more than probably random, the old hound seems to sport an air of grim satisfaction as he limps away.

Inside what we shall inevitably call the Good Intent, the decor is as hybrid as the exterior. If it were human, this bar would be suffering from an identity crisis. The owner has clearly been unable to make up his mind whether to try to recreate an English country-style pub on foreign soil, or go for what he thinks a traditional French rural bar should look like.

The heavily papered walls are dressed with a selection of agricultural implements which pre-date the old tractor I saw earlier today, and I wonder what a local farm worker would make of the idea of displaying a broken-handled slurry pit shovel as a fashionable ornament. There is a deep-pile red carpet where sensible tiles would normally be found, and the standard French high-rise bar is festooned with a line of British beer pumps. On the wall behind the bar is a sign declaring that Every Hour is a Happy Hour in this establishment, but the man standing directly beneath the notice has obviously not read it. He is leaning on the counter, looking morosely at a corner table where an attractive young woman sits talking animatedly with a man in a suit. As the suit is of only one colour, I assume the man is English or from an urban area of France. The couple's heads are close together, and though there is an open briefcase and some sheets of paper on the table, I suspect they are discussing more than a business affair.

I turn back to the man behind the bar, and see that in keeping with the general theme of his surroundings he has also made a sartorial effort to bridge the cultural gap. On his head is the first beret I have seen in this area for years, while the part of his body I can see above the bar is clad in a very British woollen sweater with leather elbow patches. He is also wearing a tie, so I greet him in English and the look of panic in his eyes subsides. Forcing a smile, he struggles manfully to appear the benevolent mine host and asks me what I will have. I see that he is looking expectantly at the range of beer pumps, and when I ask for a bottle of French beer and a pastis for my wife, he tries not to show disappointment.

While I wait for our drinks to be served, I introduce myself and ask how he came to be standing where he is. He looks as if he has been asking himself the same question for some time, then says he has heard of the couple who bought a house next to a dog kennels. As he says this, his expression lightens momentarily and I suspect this is because he is pleased to think he is not the only Briton in the area to make a disastrous mistake in property purchase. He then explains that setting up the bar was the realisation of a long-held dream for him and his wife. She is the lady sitting with the man in the corner, who is helping them make a success of the bar. The couple had been coming to France on holiday for many years and would stay at a nearby gite. They had always wanted to have a home and income in France, and when the bar and grocery store closed and the chance arose to take early retirement from his job as a Human Resources manager in Sidcup, they decided to take the plunge. The Entente Cordiale has been open for just two weeks, and his aim is to make it of equal appeal to local people, visitors, and what he calls British incomers.

I ask how the food side of the business is going and he looks even unhappier. When they started the enterprise, he says, his wife and he had intended to offer a full-scale restaurant service with a combination of classic French and British dishes on the menu. They soon learned that their French customers would not eat food cooked by a Briton at any price, and the expatriate clientele seem only interested in plates of curry or cottage pie.

I pick up our glasses, sympathise and wish him well for the future. He says he is sure that things will get better, and tries to look enthusiastic before busying himself by polishing one of the already gleaming beer pump handles. Joining Donella and Milly at a table in the corner, I tell her about the new owners of

64

the bar and their plans to create a truly cosmopolitan oasis in the hamlet. My wife looks at me and around the bar, then asks if the owner might be a distant relative of mine. I start to ask why she should think this, then realise she is being waspish.

I appreciate that the road to Hell and financial catastrophe for many Britons who set up bar and restaurant businesses in France is paved with good intentions, but still admire the owner and his wife for what they are trying to do. I have my doubts that local people will ever be attracted to the idea of trying a glass of Ramsbotham's Old and Peculiar ale with a helping of anglicised curry, but the Entente Cordiale should appeal to many of the Britons now living in the area. Although most would say they came here to get away from Britain, we are all most comfortable in familiar surroundings and it is often the everyday things we miss most. This is not exclusive to the British temperament, as anyone who has seen a Frenchman looking at a sliced loaf in an English supermarket will know. Arriving at Cherbourg some years ago, I saw a man kneel and kiss the quayside as his fellow French travellers applauded. Moments later and accompanied by raucous cheering from his friends, a very drunk British youth fell headlong down the gangplank, cut his head quite badly and bled profusely on the sacred soil of France. This little tableau seemed to sum things up nicely *vis a vis* our respective cultures and their general views of foreign travel.

There is a recent edition of an English newspaper on our table, and flicking through it I note that not much seems to have changed during our absence from Britain. A full-page advertisement offers refrigerators the size of wardrobes and gas cookers with double ovens, plate warmers, supercharged grills and up to seven burners for their buyers not to use. It is, I think, a particularly curious modern paradox that the less frequently people cook proper meals at home in Britain, the bigger and better equipped and more expensive they feel their kitchens must be.

Elsewhere an entire page is dedicated to how women readers may determine what type of backside they have. According to the preamble, a psychology professor has devised a formula for the perfect shape and size, with various equations determining characteristics such as bounce, symmetry and texture. Having presumably done his homework and research, the professor forecasts that Australian pop singer Kylie Minogue would almost certainly score a perfect eighty points for her pert bottom. Having set the test, the author of the article then goes on to suggest what female readers should wear to either disguise or flaunt their type of arse. A note at the bottom of the piece somewhat cheekily observes that, applying the formula to other members of the animal kingdom, the greater red-buttocked baboon scores nearly as many points as the Antipodean chanteuse.

I look at the date at the top of the page to check it is not the First of April, then move on to a story about a British couple emigrating to Normandy whose pet rabbits were banned from travelling on a French ferry. The couple's dog, goat, tortoise, snake and tarantula spider were welcome passengers, but not the two giant lop-eared albinos, which are, perversely, a French breed. In the article, the company's suitably embarrassed public relations officer explains that all French sailors have a superstitious dread of carrying rabbits because of a tragic incident in the 17th century. According to the legend, a rabbit escaped from the larder of a warship and gnawed its way through the keel causing the vessel to sink with the loss of all lives. Since then and in the manner that the mention of *Macbeth* is shunned by British thespians, even the word *lapin* is considered taboo in French seafaring circles.

The article concludes with a listing of other French superstitions. I see that it is considered very unlucky to cross a stream while carrying a cat, and that a swallow alighting on one's shoulder is a harbinger of death. These two beliefs seem quite logical, as most cats I know would object quite strongly to being picked up and carried over water. Also, as it is said that swallows spend every moment of their brief lives in the air I should imagine that one falling from the sky and on to your shoulder would be a reliable indicator of a death in the vicinity.

Having checked that the list of French ill-omens does not include the purchase of a proposed holiday camp next door to a dog kennels, I show the article to my wife. When I remark how curious it is that we consider a rabbit's foot lucky, Donella observes that, given traditional anglo-franco relationships, the French tragedy may be exactly why this belief came about in Britain.

We then discuss the apparent illogicality of some common proverbs and aphorisms on either side of the Channel, and I quote the French axiom that a salt-beef eater needs no candle in the cellar to find his wine. Donella defends the proverb as being self-explanatory, then reminds me that we do not query why anyone - apart from a fisherman - would want to buy a can of worms, let alone open one.

Our conversation draws some strange looks from our host, and I am about to return to my newspaper when the door opens and a new customer arrives. He is alone, but acts as if he has a companion.

An otherwise unremarkable character, he appears to be of average height and build, though is probably taller than he looks. This is because he has a pronounced stoop, and taken together with his expression of melancholia, he seems to believe he is carrying a considerable burden on his bowed shoulders. As we watch, he holds the door open and gives a gruff command. Apparently satisfied when nobody enters, he closes the door and walks across to the bar. He is obviously a regular, as no words are exchanged while the owner of The Good Intent reaches for a glass and fills it with ale. Putting the glass in front of his customer, he then produces a bowl and fills it from a water tap beneath the counter. The man nods silently, takes the bowl and places it by his feet.

Becoming aware we are watching him, the man comes across to our table after instructing the bowl to stay where it is.

On arrival, he tells me that I am not only sitting in his seat but also reading his newspaper. I start to compose a suitable reply, but a look from Donella persuades me to show better manners than he, so I apologise and offer him the paper and the seat.

Apparently mollified, he sits down alongside me and calls for the water bowl to join us. Even though we are in the mysterious marshlands of Lower Normandy I am unsurprised when it does not move, and discreetly move my chair away from the stranger. The man sees my action and explains that he was not speaking to the bowl, but calling his dog. I look at my wife and move my seat a little further away before reaching down and vaguely patting the place where I imagine he thinks the imaginary dog must be sitting. The man frowns and asks what I am doing, and when I ask him the breed of his pet he snorts and says that anyone can see there is no dog, but if I am interested, Scotty is a top-of-the-range pedigree English terrier.

Obviously pleased to have someone to talk to, he tells us his name is Eric, and that he has lived alone in a nearby village since his wife divorced him for living in Birmingham. When I say that even to people who have been to Birmingham that would seem unreasonable grounds for divorce, he says I do not know his wife. She did not like the city and wished to move away, but he had refused to pay the hugely inflated prices of property in other parts of the country. She cited his extreme meanness as the reason for claiming her freedom, and tried to claim all his money as well. With what was left after the settlement, he moved to Normandy where property was still a reasonable price. His only companion had been the family dog, which his wife had not liked. Sadly, the dog had died a month ago. Missing the animal but not missing all the overheads, he had read a story in a newspaper about a new fashion for 'virtual pets' in Japan and America. The puppies exist only in a computer game, but look and behave like real animals. They can allegedly be stroked, taught to recognize their owner and can catch fleas and even defecate. The huge advantage to the millions of owners is that there are no vets bills or need to walk their charges, and unlike the real thing, the Nintendogs keep themselves happy on their own for hours on end. The disadvantage to the otherwise good idea, Eric quickly realised, was that he did not have a computer, and the cost of buying one and the necessary programming would far exceed the price of a real dog. Then, inspiration struck. If he invented the virtual-virtual dog, he would have all the advantages of the computerised version and none of the drawbacks of the real thing.

Unlike his former wife, Scotty is obedient and affectionate and best of all, costs nothing to keep. Unlike our mongrel, his dog is an expensive breed and would have cost a small fortune if real. Eric concludes his tale by suggesting that we might think about following his example and getting rid of our cross-breed. Returning to Donella the cautionary look she gave me earlier, I say that it is an interesting idea, and suggest I get in a virtual round of drinks.

As we drive away from The Good Intent, I observe that the idea of an imaginary pet is not such a bad one. My wife sniffs caustically and says she thinks the idea of a virtual husband a better one. However imaginary he was, he could hardly be worse at earning a living than me.

To say a leek is the asparagus of the poor
is to be impolite to the leek, the asparagus and the poor.

Albert Valentin

6

Three days before the deadline.

It is the time of full moon, and last night my sleep was disturbed by an unearthly howling. I sent Donella next door to complain, but Mr Querville claims the noise was our cat celebrating another assault on their monstrous pet. Our neighbour says he does not wish us to fall out, but if we do not stop Lupin terrorising his dog he is going to report us to the mayor. He also threatened to tell the local hunting society about the ferocious creature roaming the *marais* after dark and warn them they will need to load their rifles with silver bullets. He says he is a Basque so understands these things, and our cat is possessed of an evil spirit. Donella said she finally placated Mr Querville by agreeing to keep Lupin indoors until the moon wanes, and we have been invited to their home for drinks tomorrow evening. It will be, she points out, an opportunity for us to build bridges and demonstrate to our new neighbour that, unlike our cat, we are fairly civilized.

*   *   *   *   *

This afternoon we are meeting with Mr Lecroix to ask him to declare the sale of Le Marais unsound, but before then I have to correct a mistake made by our new postman.

The bright yellow van arrived in our yard just after breakfast and released the cadaverous and unusually lofty *facteur*. Apart from his height, Thierry the Tall differs from our previous postmen in other more surprising regards. When I invited him in to the house for a break, he primly announced that he neither smokes nor drinks, which is most unusual in my experience of rural French postmen. He also refused to be drawn when I asked about any scandal going on in the area, which in my experience of rural French postmen is unique.

After seeing our uncommunicative postman off and opening an innocent-looking envelope, I was shocked to see it was a threatening letter from a bank. I have become used to these across our years in France, but had not realised that after the sale of La Puce we could already owe so much interest on our loan. Nor that we were so far behind with the repayments.

My first thought was that our new bank manager has heard about me and written a rehearsal letter which had been posted by mistake. When I had taken a reviving glass of last year's blackberry port, I found Donella in the henhouse and showed her the letter. She looked at it briefly then pointed out that it was actually addressed to a lady in a hamlet some miles away and came from a bank with which we had never done business. As she said, even we could not owe money to a bank with which we did not have an account. The name on the envelope is Lady West, so our postman had made an understandable mistake. Having two foreigners with cardinal points for names could easily lead to confusion, even if we do have different postcodes. As the envelope was marked urgent and I needed to occupy myself until our meeting with Mr Lecroix, it would be a kindly thought to take it to its rightful owner.

I agreed, and said it would also give me a chance to meet an English aristocrat while exploring our new area further. I didn't say that the exploration would also be an opportunity to look for suitable properties to rent, or that it would also be interesting to meet someone who seems to be even worse at managing their financial affairs than me.

*   *   *   *   *

I have arrived at the West household by a very convoluted route. There are degrees of remoteness in rural France, and our near-namesake really does live in the middle of nowhere. The nearest hamlet to her home is not shown on the map, and there are no road signs or other official indicators that this part of the marshlands is inhabited. This may be helpful to locals who do not wish to be registered with the authorities, but a problem for any stranger to the area. In my travels today, I have also re-confirmed the pointlessness of asking directions in rural France.

To begin with, it is extremely difficult to even explain where you are trying to get to as all villages and hamlets have their own carefully contrived pronunciation for their and every other settlement in the area. This tradition may have come about by people wishing to identify with their neighbours or distance themselves from the outside world, or perhaps it may be just out of momentary spite because you, as a foreigner, have actually pronounced the name properly. Added to this, there is the problem of the person you ask not actually having heard of your destination, which is not uncommon even if it is only a mile down the road from where he or she grew up. Being a severe loss of face to admit ignorance of the area to an outsider, it is quite likely that you will be sent off in completely the wrong direction.

But I have finally arrived. Finding the front door to the

house leaning against a disused well in the yard and considering the overall condition of the cottage, I assume that Lady West has not built up her massive overdraft in building repairs and improvement costs. In my years in rural France I have come across some spectacularly distressed yet occupied buildings, but the owner of this one seems to have taken dilapidation to almost an art form.

Seeing no bell or knocker on the disembodied door, I walk into the dark interior of the cottage and call a greeting, then step back sharply as a figure in what looks like a nuclear decontamination suit shuffles down the passage towards me. The inside of the cottage, I assume, must be even more potentially hazardous than the outside.

After a muffled greeting, the wearer lifts the visor of what I now see to be a welding mask, shakes off one of her asbestos gauntlets, apologises for the shock she has given me, then introduces herself. The elderly, pleasant-faced lady apologises for the sticky deposit left on my hand and reassures me it is only honey. As we go into the cottage, she explains that she finds the helmet, overalls and gloves are more effective than the standard bee-keepers protective clothing, and cost much less. She also bought a very cheap welding kit with the outfit, and has enjoyed learning how to use it by turning the old Citroen van in the yard into an open-top saloon.

Reaching what I assume is the living room, my elderly hostess begins to strip, and I am grateful to see that she is fully dressed under her overalls.

When she has persuaded one of at least six small dogs to make space on the sofa, she asks me to excuse the mess and says it is the cleaner's year off. Unsure if she is joking, I sit down and hand her a ham sandwich in an interesting state of decomposition while accepting her offer of a glass of pumpkin surprise brandy. When I ask how the name of her home-made liqueur came about, she says she was surprised how drinkable it is, given its appearance and what went into the making of it.

While Lady Babs finds and busies herself with a collection

of former lemonade bottles on a table in the corner, I sit back and think about how lucky I am to meet so many interesting and unusual people. As in the wilder areas of Cornwall, Wales and Scotland, this part of Normandy seems to have a particular attraction for dedicated non-conformists. Most people of this woman's age would be sitting resignedly in an old people's home waiting for the end. But Barbara West chooses to live alone in an isolated cottage in a foreign land, and is obviously determined to ignore the depredations of the passing years along with the cleaning and house repairs.

She returns from the sink and I take the tumbler of the murky liquid. Though it is not actually smoking sulphurously, I am careful not to spill any on sensitive parts of my skin. I shut my eyes and take a sip, and find it tastes much better than it looks, which, on reflection, it would have to. When I regain my breath and compliment her on the smoothness, she confesses she discovered the recipe by accident while making pumpkin soup and trying to enhance the flavour with a whole range of unusual additives. As well as being a pleasant drink, she finds the potion excellent as a clearer of blocked drains, and a perfect solution in which to steep her dentures overnight.

Removing a small and inquisitive puppy from my pocket, I hand her the letter from the bank manager and say the postman must have confused our surnames. She says that this is a not uncommon problem, and I discover that Thierry is technically as unsuited to his job as any one-armed bricklayer. It seems that as well as lacking a taste for alcohol, tobacco and gossip, our mutual postman suffers from chronic dyslexia. Having so many families on his round with the same name does not help, but Thierry's impediment is actually seen as a benefit by some residents. By receiving other people's mail, locals can keep themselves abreast of what is happening in their neighbour's lives without having to rely on gossip, which is by its nature often ill-informed.

After refilling our glasses, Barbara scans the letter and the attached statement of how much money she does not have in the bank, then shrugs and throws it on the fire. As we sit and watch the paper curl and singe before bursting into flames, I say I wish all money problems could be disposed of so easily. She smiles grimly and says that the bank will have a problem recouping their money before she rejoins her husband.

As she speaks I notice her look fleetingly at a framed photograph on a bureau in one corner of the chaotic room. The photograph is of a couple sitting outside a bar, and I see what a beauty Lady Barbara was in her youth. In contrast to its surroundings, the bureau is immaculately polished and has the only clearly uncluttered surface in the room. In front of the picture are a single wild flower and a greetings card. Lifting her chin, my hostess says her husband left her almost two years ago, and yesterday would have been his birthday. I look at my feet and mumble something inappropriate, and she explains he died in this house after an unexpected heart attack. Although all heart attacks are by their nature unexpected, her husband was so full of life and never ill, and their friends would often say what a hale and hearty chap he was. After the funeral, she felt she could not go and leave him alone in a country where they had shared such good times. He had been a wonderful husband and man, but not good at business or at providing for the future. The bank has been trying to make her sell the cottage, but she has ensured that it does not seem an attractive proposition to the few would-be buyers who have dared to enter the hole where the front door was. Friends also alerted the regional newspaper to her situation, and they have made a fuss about a grasping bank trying to steal the home of a widow whose aristocratic husband fought so bravely alongside the Resistance during the war. In fact, says Barbara, her husband spent the war years in charge of a catering supplies depot in North Yorkshire, but she didn't like to spoil the story for the readers, or let the bank manager off the hook.

*   *   *   *   *

An absorbing hour passes as Barbara tells me of her eventful times and travels with her husband, and I am comforted to hear of a couple who have taken on life so vigorously and got by without worrying overly about money. I look at the clock on the mantelpiece, and after regretfully refusing another glass of the pumpkin brandy, explain that our appointment with Mr Lecroix is in less than an hour and I still have to find my way home.

We walk out to the yard and I stroke a friendly goat as Barbara gives me directions for a short cut back to Le Marais and relative civilisation. I ask her if she ever feels lonely and she smiles and says of course she does, but she has her animals to keep her company, and a French widow of her age lives no more than a mile away. They lunch together every day, and go to town once a week to get disgracefully tipsy and flirt with the skirt-chasing owner of the Bar du Bon Parle. Neither he nor she would be interested in any actual dalliance, of course, but at her age it is nice to be asked.

As she speaks, Lady Barbara runs her hand down her face and looks wistfully into the past, and on an impulse I lean forward and kiss her weathered cheek. She stiffens for a moment, then steps away and takes out a rumpled handkerchief and blows her nose loudly. Dabbing at her eyes, she tells me that I remind her very much of her late husband. He was a big man in size and spirit, and the sort of person who did not let things get him down for long. As one gets older, it is important to remember that life flies by, and if we are lucky enough to find a soul mate we must cherish every moment we are allowed to be together.

I tell my new friend that my mother gave me exactly that advice when I was too young to heed it, then impulsively step forward and put my arms around her. We stand there for a moment as the goat nibbles at its mistress's skirt and an elderly rooster comes strutting around the corner of the cottage to see what is going on. After thinking how lucky I am and how quickly life goes by, I promise to become a regular caller, and carefully nursing a bottle of pumpkin surprise, climb into my car.

As I drive away, the sound of a familiar dull thud echoes down the lane. I stop and run back to see my new friend holding a shotgun aloft. She sees me and my expression, laughs and then explains. It is her turn to make lunch, and as she has no telephone, the firing of the shotgun is the signal to her distant friend that the *pot-au-feu* is ready. There is no fear of her signal being confused with firing elsewhere in the vicinity, as no French hunter would be either capable of or contented by killing his prey with a single shot.

Driving away from the tumbledown cottage and its redoubtable owner I think how a hundred or more years ago, British ladies of Barbara's age and character would be striding purposefully up the banks of the Limpopo in a heavy and very unsuitable full-length skirt whilst scorning the climate, unfriendly natives and animals. It is somehow reassuring to think that Barbara's kind still exist, and I think I would rather have her at my side in a tight situation than most men I know.

*   *   *   *   *

When kept waiting, the French often say they have been planted and left like a leek. For the third time in a fortnight I find myself sitting like a vegetable in an unremarkable office with an impressive clock.

We are waiting to see the notary and hopefully persuade him that the sale of La Puce should be declared unsound and that we can claim back our deposit. Looking around the waiting room more closely than during our previous visit, I think we may have our work cut out. On the table beside me is a pile of magazines devoted to hunting with dogs. The walls are lined with paintings and photographs of dogs, and a large hunting hound is taking its ease in a basket by the receptionist's desk. On the desk itself, a puppy is investigating the contents of a filing tray. From beyond the door leading to his office comes an occasional yap. One of the photographs on the wall shows our new notary sitting with the dog and proudly holding a litter of puppies. Given the evidence, I think it unlikely that Mr Lecroix would consider a dog kennels next door to one's house as a reasonable cause for concern.

*   *   *   *   *

I am driving us to drink, and it will not be to celebrate the result of our meeting with the notaire.

A large and rumpled man who looks more like a country vet than a legal executive, Mr Lecroix seems a good man in spite of his decision on our purchase of Le Marais. He is certainly an animal lover, and when we finally entered his office, he spent the first ten minutes of our meeting asking me about English breeds of hunting dog. He also mentioned how much he admires English marmalade, and I promised to have a crate of luxury preserves shipped over from a specialist grocery company in Dundee. Unfortunately, my subtle attempt to win him over had no effect on his ruling.

While sympathising with our position, Mr Lecroix says he can see no reason for cancelling our purchase of Le Marais. There may have been a legal duty for the estate agency to tell us about the kennels, but that is a matter between us and them. It was our duty to make reasonable enquiries about our neighbours, and neither the agency nor the owner of the property appears to have deliberately concealed the presence of the kennels from us. The sale is sound and must by law go ahead. When I asked bitterly if he would buy a house next door to such a place, he gave a non-committal Gallic shrug and said the kennels were there when we arrived to view Le Marais. When I asked what would happen if we refuse to sign the *Acte Finale* and offered to pay the owner compensation if our deposit is returned, he shrugged even more expressively and said it would and could not be as simple as that. He had already talked to Georges about the situation, and he and his wife are not prepared to let us withdraw at this stage. What is more, if we do refuse to go ahead with the purchase, it could cost us a lot more than a lost deposit.

Under yet another French property law of which I had not heard, as well as keeping our deposit the owners of Le Marais can also sue us for all the money they have spent based on the understanding that they had sold their home. Consequently, Georges has submitted a list of costs which include the move to their new home, improvements on his tin shed across the lane from Le Marais, and even - inexplicably - the purchase of a new underground hunting bunker on the marshlands. The total amount comes to more than sixty thousand euros, and that, as Mr Lecroix pointed out, does not allow for the deposit we would lose.

So our options are quite clear. We either go ahead and complete the purchase of the property, or refuse and lose our deposit...and will be sued by Georges into the bargain. Repeating the not-so-subtly veiled warning from the property law expert we saw last week, Mr Lecroix stressed that the case could take a very long time to be resolved, and that we should bear in mind that the plaintiff is a French national. He most sincerely advised us to appear for the signing of the *Acte Finale*, or we could learn a very hard lesson indeed.

*   *   *   *   *

Although it is early in the evening, The Good Intent is busy. In spite of its schizophrenic décor, I feel somehow at home as I wade through the crowd of British settlers taking advantage of the opportunity to get together and complain about their host country.

We have come to the English-run bar at my suggestion

and because, however irrationally, I feel I have been betrayed by the country and people I have grown to love over the years. While I am wounded, I want to be amongst my own kind. As they say, nobody wants to be ill or to die in a foreign country. But it does not take me long to remember that although we are of the same race, I speak a different language from most of the customers at The Good Intent.

I am pleased for the owners that business is brisk, and that we are here during such a busy session. As well as helping me forget our problems with Le Marais, I shall be able to observe my fellow countrymen and women at close quarters as they relax. The French novelist Marcel Proust liked to watch from afar, but I prefer to be in amongst the action when reflecting on the vagaries of human behaviour. With so many expatriate customers, this bar should provide rich pickings for my continuing study of what sets one race apart from another. Napoleon said that if three English people were washed up on a desert island their first decision would be to form a club. Whatever the intentions of the owners of The Good Intent, his clientele are demonstrating that, however much we protest the truism, every race generally likes to keep its own company.

Nowadays, Britons come to live in France for a variety of reasons, and not all of them based on sound reasoning. At one time most British settlers made the move simply because they liked the country and culture, and wanted to be part of it. Increasingly, it seems that many British expatriates are either refugees or economic migrants. The refugees say they are fleeing from the accelerating decline of standards and general quality of life in Britain. In many cases, the grass seems greener on this side of the Channel simply because the voluntary émigrés do not speak French and choose to live in the remotest of areas. In a small rural community, they are insulated from not only what is going on in their own country, but also what is going on in France.

Generally unconcerned by what is happening in either country, the economic migrants are here because of the explosion in property prices in Britain. Many of the older settlers have realised they can sell their house in Britain, buy one in France and have enough left in the bank to allow a modest existence in a country in which they would otherwise not have chosen to live. The problem for many of these people is that they can never return home unless there is a spectacular collapse of property values in the UK, or an even more spectacular hike in French house prices.

Then there is the growing influx of younger British settlers, who simply could not afford a home in Britain at any price. Like pioneers seeking a better land and future, they load up their belongings and set out across the Channel full of hope and enthusiasm. Some will come to grief, but those with the heart and adaptability will settle down and bring new blood to otherwise dying rural communities. This arrival of people from overseas in search of a better life has been happening in Britain for centuries, so I do not see why it should not happen here. But as in Britain, some people in France do not want or welcome new blood and ideas. Sometimes, I can see just why some ordinary people of the host nation are not too keen on welcoming some intending settlers or even visitors.

My progress to the bar is impeded by three women who have drawn up a defensive line of stools and handbags. In the moments it takes to break through the *cordon sanitaire*, I learn they are on holiday in the area and that one hates her job and her husband, another hates her neighbours, and that the third hates her bottom and breasts and has had a brass ring inserted in a very intimate part of her body. I learn these things not because I deliberately eavesdrop on their conversation, but because even though they know they are in a British bar, the women are also in a foreign country so naturally believe that nobody will be able to hear or understand them.

Eventually breaching the female redoubt, I find the patron pretending to listen to a lecture about the shortcomings of French cuisine and in particular the insipid quality of the tomato sauce in cans of baked beans. Our host has the look of a man listening to a variation on a theme with which he is well familiar, and nods and grunts obligingly at regular intervals as he toys with an empty glass. The bean aficionado is a stout man of late middle-age with iron-grey hair and a very red face; I can only guess as to whether the colour is his natural complexion or the result of high blood pressure brought about by his obsession with the viscosity of French baked bean sauce. After waiting for the man to pause for a breath and take a deep draught from a glass of wine that is only marginally less red than his face, I order our drinks and ask our host where his wife is. A shadow passes across Simon's face as he says that Saskia is with their friend and business associate Roger, who is giving her some lessons in business French. Remembering the closeness of the couple in the corner during my last visit, I decide not to make any flippant remarks or bad puns, and turn away to find my wife. I immediately realise I have turned the wrong way, as the florid-faced man catches my eye and begins a tirade about the inefficiencies of the French postal service. After a moment I realise that he is not talking to me but at the bar in general, so feel free to nod vacuously and make my escape as he becomes quite misty-eyed while recalling cheerful and obliging posties on red bicycles making two deliveries a day in his village in the Cotswolds. As I thread my way through the crowd to where Donella is sitting, I wonder if the puce-complexioned settler has the same postman as us. Even if he does, if he believes the British postal service better than the French he has obviously lived abroad for a long time.

Edging past a table where a group of irate men are enjoying themselves complaining about the lack of eatable sausages in France, I also wonder why we call Britons who live in a foreign country ex-patriots when so many of them seem to become much fonder of what they have left behind the longer they live abroad.

Arriving at a table near the door, I find my wife trying to look interested as Lonely Eric tells her about the latest bargains at his supermarket. I notice that Donella is becoming so bored that she is stroking the space where Eric's invisible dog is supposedly sitting. Not wishing to interrupt, I turn my attention to a nearby couple who seem to be doing their best to become one person.

Unlike the young couple at the restaurant in Sourciéville, their desire to blend into a single entity seems to be for reasons of comfort rather than passion. They have obviously been together a long time, and choose to declare their unity by appearance, expression and mannerisms. Both wear casual woollen tops and carefully pressed trousers of the same design and colour, and both have the same air of contented quiescence. Occasionally, they look around the room with an air of polite interest, after which they smile at each other as if at some shared secret. I suppose some people would mock them for their unquestioning affection for and reliance on each other, but I suspect they have discovered an easy and contented companionship which is found by very few couples.

Not wishing to learn about today's special offers at the Sourciéville Super U, I introduce myself and ask the couple if they live locally. After saying that they have heard about the English couple who bought the house next to the dog kennels, the man tells me that their French home is just down the road, but the Entente Cordiale is not their local bar, which is in a village in the Alps. I am even more interested to find that their local restaurant is in the Loire Valley, and that their local bakery in Burgundy is, in their opinion, the best in all France.

When pressed for an explanation, Phil and Phyllis say they have spent the last ten years looking for a holiday home in France. During that time, they viewed hundreds of properties in dozens of regions, but always found something not to their liking about the house or the area. Sometimes there were the right number of rooms, but the kitchen was too small. Sometimes the house came up to their specifications, but was too near a road or too far away from the nearest town. Sometimes, the property criteria were fulfilled, but the house was sadly in the wrong part of France. Another problem was that they had found something admirable in many areas, and were being driven mad by the disappointment of all their favourite places being so far apart. Eventually, they realised that they would never find their dream holiday home and location, and would have to settle for second best or give up their search. Then, travelling dejectedly back to the ferry port at Cherbourg for the hundredth time, they had stopped off at the bar, met Eric and his virtual dog, and realised they could follow his example.

If they could not find the perfect holiday home, they would simply invent one. Taking all the best features from all the houses they had seen, they had constructed their imaginary cottage in this hamlet. There was a shortage of spectacular scenery and facilities and had not the best of climates, but it was very handy for the ferries. While engaged in the virtual furnishing of their new home, they had realised they were now able to endow the area with all the best features and facilities they had encountered in their travels. So, as far as they were concerned, they now had a holiday home which cost nothing to maintain, and which was surrounded by their favourite facilities and locations. By creating their imaginary home here, they would have somewhere to visit every year and become as familiar with and to the locals as if they actually owned a property in the area.

And there were other advantages to their simple scheme. Though not regular drinkers, they were celebrating this evening as they had just heard that the price of properties in this area had risen sharply in recent months, making their virtual home even more valuable. So pleased were they with their new property and its increased value that they were considering adding an imaginary extension.

Opening and closing my mouth several times and then thinking about what has been happening in our lives recently, I congratulate the happy pair on their achievement and go to order a round of drinks. As my wife observes when I tell her the couple's story, there is something to be said for the idea, as even I would not be likely to site an imaginary dog kennels next to an imaginary ideal home.

*   *   *   *   *

We left the virtual holiday home owners making a fuss of Eric's virtual dog and took a slow and reflective drive back to Le Marais. Discussing our evening at The Good Intent, I said I was pleased to have learned a little more about people and their diverse natures. Donella said she has reminded herself of why she often prefers the company of animals to humans.

Now, my wife is saying goodnight to our chickens and I am walking Milly beside the river which winds past Le Marais and through the plain on its way to Sourciéville and the sea. Although I am normally the most gregarious of people, I prize these moments when I can be completely alone with nature. The Swiss psychiatrist Carl Jung said that if every 'civilized' person could get in touch with his or her primitive side for just five minutes a day, he would have no patients. It is one of the very few of his sayings which I understand, and one with which I totally agree.

The moon has only just begun to wane and the big Norman sky is mostly untroubled by cloud. The occasional puff of cotton wool drifts slowly across the starry ceiling, and the French would call it *un ciel moutonné*, or a sky full of sheep.

All in all, it has been a strange day. Seeing the owner of the British bar so unhappy and the couple so contented with their imaginary home has made me think about the nature of reality, why we do what we do, and how responsible we are for what happens to us.

As I understand it, there are two broad philosophical views of the game of life and how we fare in it. One side claims we are the authors of every aspect of our lives, while the other

86

claims that the Fates control our destiny, wriggle on the hook as we may. Nobody can ever know which if either school of thought is true, but blaming bad luck or fate seems a lot easier than blaming oneself for a major cock-up. Perhaps fate has brought us to this point of our lives, and has a good reason for so doing. Perhaps living next door to a dog kennels may turn out to be not such a bad experience. Perhaps, as Donella said when we had our most recent row, I have actually brought the situation about to give me something dramatic to write about. Whoever or whatever is responsible for our current circumstances, we still have a lot to be thankful for and I suspect there are a few million people on the planet who would like to be in my shoes, soggy as they are at the moment.

I am distracted from my philosophical meanderings as Milly stiffens and lifts her head from the patch of reed grass she has been investigating. As I make reassuring noises, I see she is staring intently at a clump of scrub on the other side of the stream. Something stirs, and I make out a dark shape and eyes that glitter sharply in the moonlight. For a moment I think my recent dream has become reality and the devil-dog from over the fence has begun to stalk me. Then the creature lopes casually to the bank and sits on its haunches facing us, and I see that it is only a fox. It sits and looks at us across the narrow stretch of water with typical incurious regard, and I wonder if it is the same animal we saw on our first night at Le Marais. I will never know, as all foxes look alike, especially in the dark.

As we contemplate each other, I can see that the fox is small and delicately formed, so probably a bitch, and looks well-fed and healthy. The living will have been easy during the summer months, but come the winter she will need to use all her cunning to stay alive and tend her family. The hunters will not pose so much of a problem as hunger, and nine out of ten *vulpes vulpes* starve to death in hard times for the countryside.

Although we keep chickens, I like and admire foxes for a number of rational - and some completely irrational - reasons.

They are intelligent, resourceful and adaptable, and do not seem to think the world owes them a living. They also pair for life and are conscientious parents. Most of all, they are free, though must pay the price of freedom. If it survives, the red fox can live for more than seven years, but this is no thanks to the mindless people who like to kill them for no good reason.

I ease myself down onto the river bank and gently hold Milly's muzzle as human and dog and fox regard each other across the moonshiny water. Trying to send out telepathic waves of amity, I think how we share a common time and place but are divided by our species as surely as we are by this small river. I envy this creature's freedom, but not her likely fate.

Reaching slowly into a pocket, I bring out a piece of Milly's beef jerky and hold it up. My dog grizzles a muted protest, while the fox continues to look steadily at me until I throw the piece of dried meat across the water. It lands on the bank close to her, and she starts up and disappears into the scrub. Disappointed, I get to my feet and warn my dog not to bark and frighten her and her family, as they have more right to be here than us.

I shall walk this way tomorrow and see if the scrap of food has been taken. I hope it is gone, and that the pretty creature will survive the coming winter. Like us, she has her living to make and her family to care for. She, of course, will not be troubled by considerations of whether fate or self-determination will influence her short life, and I think, all things considered, that she may be better off for her lack of self-indulgent concern.

Ainsi sera, groigne qui groigne.

A favourite motto of Anne Boleyn, which roughly translates as: 'Whinge if you will, but that's how it's going to be.'

7

As if remembering the date and its duty, the weather has changed dramatically. It is colder, the rainy season has officially arrived, and the great marsh on our doorstep has become a sea of mist. The sudden change will also mean, as they like to say in rural France, that the Devil will piss on the remaining blackberry crop and make it uneatable. My wife will be unhappy that harvest time has passed, but I can at least look forward to a blackberry-free menu by Christmas.

Tomorrow is D for Decision Day, and I have still not made up my mind as to whether we should stay at Le Marais and make the best of things, or simply cut our losses and run. Donella has said that she will abide by my decision, but I know she believes we should settle here. When I complained over breakfast of another disturbed night, she rather tartly observed how strange it was that I alone of all humanity should snore so loudly while awake, and that someone so sensitive to noises in the night did not notice the thunderstorm that raged till dawn.

Unable to think of an adequate response, I said that I would leave her to the mopping up in the outbuildings while I took Milly for a walk. I am concerned that our dog is still refusing to go near the stable block, and seems generally listless. This morning she trailed behind when I went to see if the fox had taken the scraps I left out for her, and showed no signs of interest when we chanced upon our neighbour and his giant dog on the river bank.

It is the first time I have seen Mr Querville, and as he appeared through the mist I thought he might be one of the hobgoblins said to roam the marshes in search of human prey. He is very short and swarthy even by Norman standards, while his head and features are disproportionally large. He also has an interesting mosaic of gold and rotten teeth and a jockey's short, bowed legs which sit oddly with his oversized feet. He will certainly not be at risk of being blown over by the notorious Cotentin wind, and I think if he wished, he could easily use his enormous dog for personal transport.

When he told me who he was and reminded me that we are to be his guests for drinks this evening, his French seemed almost as bad as mine. He must have seen my difficulty in understanding him, as he continued our conversation as if talking to someone who was profoundly deaf, and employed a lot of unfamiliar shrug language which I assume is Basque in origin. Overall, he seems a decent man, and I hope he may be open to reason when we talk about his dogs and the noise they make. He is also quite elderly and though I would not wish him any harm or ill-health, I am hopeful he may be nearing retirement age.

Although we had not met before, he has obviously been watching me, and made several suggestions about how I could train Milly to be a proper sheep dog. When I said that we keep no sheep, he said that we should, otherwise our dog will feel unfulfilled. Keeping order is in her blood and what she was born to do, which is why she so obviously controls me in the absence of any real sheep. I pointed out that the British like to look upon their dogs as almost members of the family, at which he nodded knowingly and said he had heard about the British and their strange attitude to family life. He also asked me if it was another British custom to encourage foxes on to land where chickens are kept, but supposed I could be luring the unfortunate creature into a fatal meeting with our ferocious cat.

After wishing him a frosty good day and saying how much I was looking forward to our meeting this evening, I walked home feeling like a man who has just lost an argument and does not know why.

*   *   *   *   *

I have relayed my conversation with our neighbour to Donella, and she reminded me that she had told me what a sensible man Mr Querville is.

The rain has returned, and we have been enjoying a regular autumn ritual in the kitchen. It is not yet cold enough for heating, but my wet clothing has given me the excuse to test out one of the cavernous fireplaces at Le Marais.

As my long shorts steamed on the back of a chair, we sat and thought about the generations of people who would have clustered around this friendly hearth. The fireplace is as big as some kitchens I have seen in Britain, and would have been a centre of peace and comfort after a hard day in the fields. It would represent warmth and security and food, and be a contented gathering place for the whole family. Nowadays in many parts of the civilized world the fireplace has been replaced by a television set, but I know which I believe to give the better entertainment and pictures.

Sitting with a mug of Donella's vegetable and blackberry soup in front of the leaping flames and breathing in the piquant aroma of burning apple wood, wet dog and my shorts, I feel at home for the first time since our arrival. I still regret agreeing to buy Le Marais and wish we had found somewhere else to live after La Puce, but, as my wife says, it is ever easy to regret the things we have done. It is only the things we do not do that turn out perfectly.

Although I am still concerned about the viability of setting up a holiday accommodation centre here, I am finding this ancient house and its surroundings more and more seductive. Our main concern if we do decide to stay at Le Marais will not be whether I can be happy here, but whether we can persuade enough English holidaymakers that they should pay to spend a night or more alongside a busy dog kennels.

*   *   *   *   *

I have been catching up with my correspondence, and it appears that it is not only we who have been having problems with their neighbours. A reader has written from south-eastern France to say that a farmer has stolen her holiday home, and now wants to charge her and her husband to stay in it. Intrigued that this can happen even in Gascony, I read on.

Disappointed with the properties for sale in their chosen area of France, the couple had decided to buy a piece of land and build their own house on it. Lacking the experience and skills to do it themselves and having heard about potential problems with rural French craftsmen, they had decided to go for the ultimate in flat-pack assembly.

After seeing an advertisement for prefabricated homes, they selected a compact yet appealing log cabin-style building that the manufacturers said could be erected in less than a day by anyone with basic DIY skills, the right tools, and several pairs of helping hands. Even better news was that the company would deliver the composite parts of the building to anywhere in France, and could also send a team to put them together on site. Having paid a deposit on their future holiday home, the couple then went in search of a suitable location.

Introduced to a farmer in a local bar, they learned he had won planning permission on a small parcel of his land and would be happy to sell it to them. Accordingly, the couple visited the site and found it perfect. At the top of a gentle rise with splendid views of the surrounding countryside, it was near enough to the road and the farmer's house for easy access to power and water supplies, yet satisfyingly secluded. Determined to do everything right, the couple had taken all reasonable actions to ensure the staked-out plot was legally for sale and that they would be its rightful owners. After satisfying themselves that all was well, they had bought the plot then returned to England to arrange for the building to be delivered and erected. All that was needed now was a concrete base to be laid and ready for when their new home arrived on the back of the lorry. So the couple returned to France to find a local builder. Having shown him the plot, they returned home and counted the days until their holiday home would be ready for occupation.

After several weeks of daily calls to the French builder and English manufacturer, they were delighted to learn that the concrete pad had been laid and their house was safely sitting upon it. Arriving on the next ferry they could not have been more pleased with what they found. Then came the bad news.

The manufacturers had built the house on the concrete pad as instructed, and the local builder had laid the foundation in the exact centre of the staked-out plot. The problem was that the stakes had somehow shifted from their original position. The log cabin, though indisputably owned by the couple, was not standing on their land, but on that of the man who had sold them the plot. The farmer said he did not want to be unreasonable, but must insist on a token yearly ground rent. When they pointed out that they could simply have the building taken down and re-erected on their plot, their new landlord said apologetically that he could not allow access for this purpose, as the further upheaval might traumatise his cows. Neither could he sell them the land on which their house was standing, as it did not have planning permission. As long as they all agreed to keep silent about their arrangement, he was sure all would be well, and it was very unlikely that anyone in the area would inform the authorities that their home had been built on grazing land and was therefore completely illegal.

I shall respond with what I hope are some comforting words and a suggestion as to how they can play the crafty farmer at his own game. Rather than worry about the threat of prosecution, they might actually think about having a trusted French friend make an anonymous call to the mayor's office about the house and its exact location. If the full force of the law were to be employed, the house would then have to be dismantled despite the farmer's objections. As it is on his land and given the complexity of French property laws, it may even be that he has to pay for the dismantling. Also, as owners of the concrete pad, they could charge the farmer a rental for its use, or even refuse to allow the owner of the land under it to break it up unless he paid for the re-erection of the log cabin on their property.

Given my experience of French law and some farmers, I do not think the couple would win that battle, but at least they will have showed that not all English property buyers in France are completely gullible.

*   *   *   *   *

The rain has eased and I am taking Milly for another long walk to try and shake off her melancholic mood. Being mostly collie, she is highly intelligent and strong-willed. Being a female collie, she is also very manipulative. A Cornish farmer friend says that he would never own another collie bitch as he could not put up with the daily battles of will, and if he wanted to be told what to do every moment of his life he could just as easily get married. But since her refusal to enter the stable block at Le Marais, my dog's character seems to have changed.

94

Owners are generally derided for claiming that their pets understand every word that they say, but I also believe our dog has telepathic powers. Not only does she seem to know what I am thinking at any time, she also seems to understand and reflect my moods. Hopefully, her lack of energy and general low spirits result from my current unhappiness at having made yet another monumental blunder on our journey through life.

Now that we have met officially, our neighbour seems to find good reason for being near our boundary fence whenever I cross the yard, and he was lying in wait for me as I put Milly in the car. When he asked where I was going and I said I was taking my dog for a walk, he wondered if it was normal for the English to take dogs for a walk by car. When I explained that I had been told about an interesting walk round a disused gravel quarry, he nodded knowingly and said I would be joining in with the English promenade. As a Basque, he understood that I would prefer to be with my own kind in a foreign country.

As I made to leave, he said he was sorry to have seen Milly digging a hole near the door to the stable block. I asked why this should upset him, and he said that it was a well-known harbinger of death. When I tried to look concerned, he warmed to the subject and said that a dog burying a stick was also a sign that a death would surely follow. When I asked him if there were any other ominous signs I should watch out for, he said that a dog rolling in grass beneath a window was a terrible omen, and that meeting a dog while crossing a bridge was even worse. Before starting the engine, I assured him I would avoid any confrontations on any bridges at the quarry, and asked how he had learned all these canine ill-omens. Giving what I took to be a particularly mournful Basque version of the all-purpose Gallic shrug, he said he was a keen observer of dog behaviour and had noticed that whenever he read in the newspapers of a death in the region, he would recall that one of his dogs had recently dug a hole, rolled in grass or buried a stick on that very day. It was, I must agree, conclusive evidence.

I nodded and drove away, wondering if my wife might be right in her accusation that I sub-consciously involve us in situations which result in meeting the most unusual people.

*　　　*　　　*　　　*　　　*

Arriving at the quarry and having checked that there were no bridges with dogs crossing them, I could see what Mr Querville meant about the English promenade. Virtually all the cars in the main parking area wore British number plates, while a handful of French-licensed cars were drawn up in a surprisingly straight line on a ridge overlooking the quarry and its surroundings. While the British are obviously here to take the air, it looks as if the local drivers and their passengers see the activity as a purely spectator sport. Though generally thought of as insular, Normans are as interested as any other race in what they see as odd or even bizarre behaviour.

No French farmer I know would actually take his dog out for a dedicated walk, and most rural people would just not see the point. Their dogs go everywhere with them, and walking is not a popular leisure pastime in our part of France. As they have grown up trudging miles to and from school and shop and work, the idea of walking for pleasure seems almost risible to most of my country-dwelling friends.

In Britain we walk our dogs for relaxation, necessity or from a sense of duty, and sometimes for social reasons. In contrast to the place of sweat and toil it must once have been, this disused workings is now a perfect setting for the traditional daily outing to exercise their dogs, and get out of the house. From what I can see, it also gives the promenaders a chance to greet and meet or snub other expatriates.

The quarry itself is now a lake of striking emerald green, and the mountains of spoil ringing the great pit have been covered by time with grass and patches of young woodland. The

96

area around the lake is also conveniently arranged on three tiers, which clearly allows the individual dog walker to select and keep to what he or she believes to be his or her proper level. In this pleasant setting I see that the British class system is on verdant display, and the French are enjoying the show.

Even from this distance, I can tell that the highest tier is the domain of those who consider themselves country and county gentry, and many of the walkers wear green Wellingtons and expensive sporting topcoats. Most seem to own Labradors, and are demonstrating their countryside skills by giving sharp commands and whistles which their dogs are ignoring with relish.

On the second level the walkers are rather formally dressed for the occasion, and one woman is wearing a fur coat and picking her way along the rough track in what appear to be high heeled shoes. Curiously, all the walkers on this level have their mostly small and well-groomed dogs tethered on leads.

At the bottom of the structure is a much more eclectic mix of walkers and dogs. All are dressed sensibly for the time of year and weather conditions, and several are carrying umbrellas. Some of the older men are declaring their individuality with large hats, long overcoats and greying pony-tails, while others look as if they are on their way to the local shop. The dogs on this level are as varied in appearance as their owners, and mingling as freely with their fellows as those on the higher tiers are not. I have no hesitation in selecting my favoured place to walk with Milly, and it will be amongst the lower ranks.

As I park alongside a car with local licence plates, I see that those inside are taking an early lunch. The French like to eat in what they call the full air, and often in what we would think of as unusual places. In general, they like to feel involved with what is going on around them, and it is not uncommon to see quite elaborate parties taking place on the edge of very busy roads; I suspect that the only reason many Normans I know do not choose to enjoy a *picnique* on the hard shoulders of motorways is because they would have to pay the toll charge to get there.

The occupants of the little Renault have obviously chosen to eat in this tranquil setting because of the chance it gives them to observe and comment on the impenetrable peculiarities of the British at play. Like a family gathering at a local soccer match, they are enjoying the food, company and the sport. In the back seat, a very excited man is using a half-eaten baguette to point at where a young woman in a track suit is running along the top tier and appears to be trying to lose her overweight Retriever. After a few vain attempts to overtake or even keep up with its mistress, the dog stops and then flops onto its belly. The woman seems unaware of the rebellion, and actually increases her pace. To the obvious amusement of the spectators in the car, she is wearing what looks like a heavy rucksack on her back and is carrying weights in her hands. They will doubtless be discussing why she should want to run away from her dog, and even more strangely, why she chose to make the job harder with such a handicap.

As the car rocks in reaction to a bout of hardcore shrugging, I see that the driver has a set of binoculars and is relaying the details of more distant events in the manner of a commentator at a horse race.

Suddenly, he lowers his field glasses and points excitedly to where the woman in the fur coat is bending over to clear up after her small terrier. When she ties the neck of the plastic bag and walks on with it dangling from her gloved hand, the car threatens to fall off its axles as the people inside react to the spectacle. In all my years in this part of the country I have never seen a French owner clear up his dog's mess, and the onlookers must believe the woman is so enamoured of her pet that she even collects and keeps the results of its bowel motions.

When I step out of my car, the man with the binoculars sees me and gives a complicitory shrug. When I fail to make a creditable response, he realises I am a performer rather than a local spectator and nudges the woman beside him. They watch expectantly as I open the back door, and when Milly leaps out and lopes off free of restraint they are clearly disappointed. They will soon have something to cheer them up, however, as I have just seen Lonely Eric emerging from a patch of woodland on the second level of the *promenade d'anglaise*. He obviously feels his imaginary dog is in need of some exercise and is throwing a stick and making encouraging signals to an empty space a few yards behind him. I point to the spot, and the driver of the Renault risks serious injury as he whips the binoculars to his eyes.

Making my way towards the lowest level of the anglicised class structure, I find my progress along the path around the lake barred by a very large mute swan. Milly has already seen the danger and taken a detour to avoid confrontation, but as I approach the bird rears up and gives the name of its breed the lie by emitting a very loud and sibilant hiss. It stalks towards me with wings outstretched and I am reminded of my recent encounter with Mr Querville's giant dog. I too take the long way round, and see that the cob's mate is lying rather forlornly amongst a patch of reeds close to the bank. It is the wrong time of year for the pen to be nesting, so her mate's over-protective manner must mean that she is injured. Like foxes, swans pair for life, and the male will take on any interloper who may try to harm or woo his mate away.

As I look at the female swan and wonder how I can help her, a large man approaches with what looks like a close relative of Milly at his heels. He says that he comes to the quarry every day and has been feeding the swans. He too believes that the female is hurt, and has arranged for a local vet to be taken by boat to treat her. It will be expensive, but he cannot bear to see such a lovely creature suffer and possibly die.

When I ask him if he lives in the area, the man says that he and his wife moved over to live near Sourciéville a year ago. He is a retired bus driver and they have no children or other ties across the Channel, so sold their house to be able to live the rest of their lives in the sort of surroundings to which they could never aspire in England. I ask him if his wife is happy to have made the move, and a shadow passes across his face as he says that she is not well. She has had the finest treatment and care imaginable at the hospital, but lately and after the treatment for her illness she does not have the energy to join him on their favourite walk. I notice he does not say from what illness his wife is suffering, and mumble my awkward condolences as he nods stiffly then looks over my shoulder at the female swan. After we have stood in silence for a little while, I say goodbye and that I hope his wife gets better soon and that I will see them on the walk together. He nods heavily again but does not reply, and I walk off to find Milly. I think I know why he is doing what he can for the swan, and that he knows his wife will never join him on the walk. As usual when I hear of such things happening, I feel at the same time selfish, lucky... and somehow guilty.

Milly and I have progressed to the middle tier of the English promenade, and I reflect on how much easier it is for a man to climb physically from one level to another than to do so in social terms. The lady in the fur coat totters by and when I greet her, she looks at me as if I have proposed rough sex rather than wishing her a good morning.

A little further along the track and I see that Milly is being pestered by the second biggest dog I have seen this week. It is obviously a very posh breed, and according to its status ranking must have come down from the upper tier to go slumming. Normally, Milly would make short work of seeing off any amorous male, but in her present downcast state she puts up little objection as the long Russian snout explores her rear end. As I consider with which boot I should explain to the intruder that his attentions are not welcome, the arrival of the dog's apologetic owner saves me the problem. He reaches down and secures his dog with what looks like a hand-crafted and plaited leash, and I realise he is the grey-haired man I saw recently in The Good Intent. As I think how his approach to the owner's wife was not a lot more subtle than that of his dog to mine, the man introduces himself and his companion. His name is Jonathan Kerr, his randy friend is called Igor, and he is walking the pedigree wolfhound as a favour to a lady friend.

I consider asking him how many lady friends he does favours for and what their husbands think of this service, but content myself with enquiring as to his profession. He tells me that he is a semi-retired business consultant specialising in property development, and came to lower Normandy some years ago on behalf of a client. His customer wished to buy and restore French country property as a long-term investment, and Jonathan had so loved the fine old buildings in the area that he had bought one for himself. He casually mentions the name of what I know to be a very grand castle on the outskirts of Sourciéville, and says that what he had intended to have been a hobby is now a full time job. He spends most of his time in this country restoring the old place, and has also been helping other Britons with their property projects.

He then asks me where I live, and I find myself telling him about our problems. After listening attentively, he claps me on the shoulder and tells me that I should cheer up. I have just taken a wrong turning and it should not be too difficult to get back on the right track. If I would like, he can send a business colleague to look at our house and situation, and if there is any way he can help a fellow Briton, he will. Taking a card from a slim leather folder, he gives it to me, shakes my hand and, after a breezy goodbye, walks off up the hill with his posh dog.

I look at the card and put it in my pocket before continuing our walk. We have still not paid the balance on Le Marais, but I will have to make up my mind by tomorrow afternoon. A lot will depend on what Mr Querville has to say about his future intentions when we meet tonight, but I think it might be helpful to have Jon Kerr as a friend. Although I suspect he is as much as a skirt-chaser as the proprietor of The

Bar du Bon Parle, he seems a decent man. My wife often accuses me of rushing to a judgment on people I meet and usually getting it wrong, but one thing I think I do very well is to instinctively determine someone's character and type.

*   *   *   *   *

We have been guests of the Quervilles, and are on our way home after an interesting though ultimately costly and disappointing evening.

It was the first time I have been on our neighbours' land, and it was a relief to find the devil-dog was not on duty at the gate. As well as dogs, our neighbours obviously have a soft spot for all manner of animals which are down on their luck, and it took almost half an hour to persuade my wife to pass by a couple of broken-down old carthorses, two nervous and badly moth-eaten goats, a duo of moulting peacocks, a pair of surprisingly anorexic pigs and the three-legged sheep and its mate. Further pairings of retired or poorly animals made themselves known through the darkness as we walked to the small single-storey building at the end of the track.

At the house, which I had half-expected to be in the shape of an ark, we were greeted by Mrs Querville. She is a homely, comfortable and shiny faced woman who must be at least a foot taller than her husband. As she explained in much better French than her husband, she is not a Basque but from a particular area of the Pyrenees where the air is thin and people grow towards the sun. Having instinctively realised that my wife shares her disposition towards all animals which are down on their luck, Madame ushered me into the presence of her husband before taking Donella on an extended tour of her menagerie.

Armed with a bottle of malt scotch, I ducked under the low doorframe and found our host sitting by the fireplace. Beside the chair and towering over his master was the monstrous hound. Close to and in the full light and small kitchen, it looked even bigger than during our previous meetings.

After taking a seat alongside Mr Querville and to break the ice, I asked the name of his dog, and he said *Zakur*. I said it was an interesting name and asked if it had any special meaning. He looked at me oddly and said it meant 'dog' in Basque. When I asked what sort of dog Zakur was, he said it was *xuriak*. When I asked what that word meant, he looked at me even more oddly and said it was Basque for 'white'. When I explained that I was asking what breed his dog was, he said that, like the Basque people, Zakur was unique. His ancestors were the result of Basque shepherds travelling to Newfoundland centuries ago, but he doubted that there was another dog in the world of the size and strength of Zakur. I agreed and suggested we open the bottle of scotch, after which the conversation eased considerably. As is invariably the case, strong drink demonstrated its ability to help each of us to understand what the other was saying. This is a phenomenon known to everyone who has found themselves increasingly fluent in a foreign language in direct proportion to the amount of alcohol consumed.

With the bottle half empty and my host more than half convivial, I broached the subject of his business and future plans. As if he had been waiting for me to bring the matter up, Mr Querville smiled craftily and said he had heard that I had heard that he was retiring soon. The rumours were true, he added, but, unless I would like to make an offer for the house and business, his son would be joining them next year to take over the running of the kennels. And their son has ambitious plans. Leaning forward and holding out his glass for a refill, he said that he understood that I was not happy to have him as a neighbour, but he and his wife and his dogs had been here for many years before we arrived. They had always done everything they could to ensure that the barking was kept to a minimum, but dogs would be dogs. He put it to me that if I bought a house next to a bar, I could hardly expect the owner to get rid of his customers so that I would not be disturbed by their noise. I agreed, but said I would probably be in the bar most of the time and be by far the noisiest of the customers, so the comparison was not an apt one.

The evening progressed more cordially as my wife and I learned a little about the history and origins of the Basque peoples and their love of nature, music, art and sport. I also learned from our host that the English word 'bizarre' comes from the Basque for beard, which perhaps explains why my neighbour regards me as more than slightly odd. Before we left, I also learned how not to play a favourite Basque card game called *mus*. As Mr Querville demonstrated, the game uses forty cards split into four families, and is based almost entirely on bluff. During an hour at the table, I discovered that my neighbour has an ideal face and mind for the game, and that, as his wife said, I do not.

After I had paid my debts and promised to teach Mr Querville how to play killer dominoes when they return the visit next week, we said our goodnights.

*   *   *   *   *

The night air is sharp and a misty rain falls, but I am well insulated. On the outside I have the padded body-warmer my wife made from an old duvet, and on the inside a mixture of the malt scotch and a selection of full-blooded wines from the southern Basque region.

We are walking back to Le Marais and discussing our visit to the Quervilles and how it will affect our decision tomorrow. Rather than be worried by their plans to expand their business, my wife sees an opportunity for us to bring in some extra income without having to put up with human guests. Instead of trying to stop the Quervilles, we should think about joining

104

them. If we offered to use our barn and stable block as extra accommodation for their boarders, we could charge per dog. We would then have some regular income, and she knows that I would prefer dogs to human guests. Donella also believes that knowing we are earning money from our neighbours will make me less sensitive to the barking. As she reminds me, I have often said that the noise of other people's dogs and children is always much more irritating than your own.

I am thinking about her proposal when we reach the gate to the courtyard and a shadowy figure moves towards us. I point my torch defensively in its direction, and the beam reveals a young man in a crimson shirt with yellow tie and a mauve three-quarter length leather coat over sodden green trousers. Taken together with the official clipboard he is carrying, the colour scheme indicates he must work for a provincial government agency.

He appears to have been waiting in the rain for some time, as his hair is plastered to his head and his wispy moustache droops despondently. As well as cold, wet and miserable, he also looks nervous, and I wonder if he has met Lupin. When I ask him if he has seen a large cat in the area, he does not reply but asks if I am Mr George West. When I correct him he looks bemused, then takes an envelope from his pocket and holds it out. Instinctively I take it, then sign the proffered clipboard. With no further comment, the man squelches hurriedly over to a small car parked outside Georges' shed and drives away. My wife and I look at each other, then I start to open the envelope, saying that our visitor was probably returning another letter which has been misdirected by our dyslexic postman. I say that I am impressed that the post office is making amends at this time of night, then shine my torch on the single sheet of paper. Beneath a very official looking crest, the document informs me that I am commanded to make an appearance at the offices of *maitre* Jean Lecroix on the following day at two p.m. prompt, or face the full rigours of the law.

We stand in the rain and look at each other again. It seems that my decision has been made for us, and if we do not turn up for the completion of the sale of Le Marais tomorrow I shall become a fugitive. In many years of sometimes sailing a little close to the wind this is the first time I have received a summons, and it looks as if, like it or not, Le Marais is to become our new home.

PART TWO

Le temps est comme un fleuve; il ne recontre pas a sa source
(Time is like a river; it does not flow back to its source)

Antoine Rivaroli, Comte de Rivarol

8

A clear, bright, morning as I watch two men struggle to free a car from the soggy grip of the marshlands. There are said to be a number of safe passages through the *marais* even when it is in full flood, and their secrets are passed on through each generation of local families. The men I am watching are either strangers, or locals who did not listen carefully enough to their parents. Although it is still early in the day, perhaps they have been celebrating their hunting trip before rather than after the event.

The car is an old Peugeot, and the more the men rock the chassis back and forward, the further the wheels sink into the morass. Being French breeds, several wild horses, a donkey and a number of the cows still out to graze have gathered to watch and enjoy the *cinema*, but are not yet giving the men advice on how best to rescue their car.

I am watching the small but entertaining drama unfold from the balcony at Le Marais, which - along with the rest of the property - has been ours since yesterday afternoon. It is a relief not to be squatting in someone else's house, but being legally summoned to the notary's office to complete the sale made it a tense and uncomfortable occasion.

After we had gone through the now familiar procedure and I had passed the cheque over and officially re-taken possession of the keys, we and the previous owners parted on the pavement after the briefest of exchanges. Watching their hunched figures scurrying away into a waspish wind, I wondered if we will be at Le Marais for as long as George and Mad lived there, and how pleased they must be to have sold their home now that Mr Querville intends expanding his business.

Oscar Wilde said there are two forms of tragedy. One is not getting what you want, and the other is getting it. With the forced purchase of Le Marais, I seem to have managed both at the same time. But what is done is done. We must now get on with our lives and make our new home pay its way, and I am looking forward to the challenge. I shall meet with an old friend at our local bar this afternoon, and he has offered to find us some reliable tradesmen to help convert the stable block into guest bedrooms. If all goes well we shall be open for business by Christmas, and though we will be employing French rural craftsmen, I am hoping that it will be this Christmas. I shall also give serious thought to my idea of marketing Le Marais as a perfect holiday destination for fanatical dog-lovers and those with chronic hearing problems.

I hear an angry buzzing in the distance, then see a figure on a moped zigzagging towards the stranded Peugeot. As he nears, I recognise the *guardien* of the marshlands, and note that Albert is wearing his official hat rather than a crash helmet. This does not bode well for the car owner and his friend if they are on the *marais* without permission.

Arriving at the battered cabriolet, Albert climbs from his moped and shakes hands with the men. It is too distant for me to see whether it is a friendly, formal or even hostile handshake, but the way the guardian of the *marais* adjusts his peak cap afterwards, I suspect the men are strangers.

Following an exchange of arm-waving and shrugging,

some agreement seems to be reached and one of the men goes to the boot and returns with a stout rope. At first I think he is going to try and lasso one of the horses, but then see Albert take the rope and begin to tie it to the pannier of his moped. Obviously, the car is so badly bogged down that he has decided that natural horsepower will not be up to the job, and that nothing short of the awesome pulling power of his moped will suffice. If that is his intention and the little machine is a classic *Mobylette*, I think he may be proven right.

For many years, this deceptively powerful two-stroke was the favourite form of transport for working people, and particularly popular in Normandy because a tank's worth of fuel can last for more than a hundred miles. The legendary durability of the *Mobylette* also makes it suitable for all manner of ancillary agricultural tasks, and I have seen fully-grown cows arrive at market in trailers pulled by one.

Times change even in rural France and most manual workers now own cars, so the company making these redoubtable machines closed down some years ago. To mark and mourn the occasion there were suitable ceremonies across France, and at our nearest town dozens of owners took part in a dignified procession through the high street. This was followed by a demonstration of trick-riding in the square, and the top prize was awarded to an eighty-year-old who ended his display with a wheelie up the steps of the town hall. After drinking the entire contents of the winner's cup, he fell off his machine twice before being helped back into the saddle and escorted home by a phalanx of police motorcycle outriders. This combination of sentimentality, sense of theatre and acknowledgement of the really important things in everyday life is another of the many reasons we like to live in the countryside of France.

*   *   *   *   *

111

The *bar-épicerie* at Sousville is typical of its genre, but like all rural bars has its own very individual character. The owner is an elderly lady who lives above the shop, and the customers buy their groceries or take a drink in one of the two downstairs rooms. As is normal with these small concerns, the shelves carry an interesting mix of provisions, and the range of goods will depend on the particular needs of the locals and what everyday items the owner can afford to stock. I have spent hours browsing in village stores across Northern France, and love to see corn plasters, shotgun cartridges and rat poison rubbing shoulders with fresh cream cakes and home-made black puddings.

Sharing the ground floor of the house, the *Bar des Amis* is more like a domestic front room than a bar. This is because it was a front room before it became a bar, and has been left almost exactly as it was before Madame bothered to formalise the situation by applying for a licence.

Like The Good Intent, the floor is carpeted, but unlike the British-owned bar, all the furniture, furnishings and ornaments are original and uncontrived and so suit their setting perfectly. There are several well-weathered but still plump armchairs for privileged customers, and a rickety dining table and mismatching chairs for those who visit in their working clothes. On top of a sideboard in one corner are silver-framed photographs of Madame's late husband and extended family, and one wall is dominated by a large portrait of General de Gaulle at his most patrician. Or as many Britons and non-Gaullists might say, at his most arrogant. There is no bar in the Bar des Amis, but a servery has been created by simply knocking a hole through the wall to the kitchen. From there, Madame Poelet dispenses drinks and discipline while creating an unending procession of traditional and local dishes at her cooking range.

Curiously and although she seems to spend most of her day at the cooker, food is not on the menu at the bar. As Madame lives alone and appears to have no bigger appetite than a small bird, I think she must cook so much for the sheer love of it – or perhaps be feeding several needy families in the village. Like the landlady at my former local, beneath her steely exterior Madame Poelet nurtures a kindly soul, and like the best philanthropists she does not advertise her charitable works. As I am English and thus a stranger to good home-cooked food, Madame is always ready to serve me up a plateful of whatever is being created on her ancient stove.

Today though, I sense that all is not well. Though all seems normal, I detect a certain stiffness amongst the handful of customers on duty. As usual at this (or any other) time of day, the three founder members of the Sousville synchronised drinking and smoking team are practicing their routine at the table beneath the serving hatch. Their act has been honed to perfection across the years, and they remind me of a Victorian mechanical curiosity as they drink and smoke in much-practised harmony. But today, the precise unison with which each lays down his cigarette and picks up his glass seems slightly out of kilter. There is hardly a heartbeat in discrepancy as each glass or cigarette touches its holder's lips, but the fractional discordancy is enough to signal that all is not as it should be.

Turning my attention to the other customers, I greet the two regulars who are occupying the armchairs that have become their exclusive domain by the international pub rules of long and established usage. Both men live in the village, are retired farmers and have been drinking here since before the bar became a bar. In this part of the world, the custom of inviting local people to have a drink in your front room while paying for the pleasure was already in force before formal licensing regulations came along.

Jules and Jacques have been drinking partners for so long that they have become as polished in their timing and delivery as the slickest double-act. Like the long-married couple I met in The Good Intent, they each seem to know what the other is thinking and have developed an impressive conversational

113

system for saving breath and energy. But today, their perfectly-timed and alternate responses have a sharp edge.

When I say hello, Jules grunts a gruff acknowledgement, and when I observe that it is becoming colder by the day, Jacques says that anyone who doesn't like the weather here should perhaps think about going back to where they came from. When I tell him that my last home was only twenty miles down the road, Jules reminds me that my real home is surely across the Channel, and only a sharp word of reproof from the kitchen prevents the conversation from deteriorating further.

I arrive at the hatch and see Madame is chopping shallots into precisely uniform rings with an almost vindictive manner. When I ask what food of the gods she is preparing, she replies that it is nothing more than cow's tongue in onion and herb gravy. I go through my usual act of pretending to faint with hunger, but for once she does not smile and ask if I would like to try a morsel. Wiping her hands briskly, she serves my drink and returns to her work while I go and sit in the corner to sulk.

Idly flicking through the pages of the local paper as I wait for my friend to arrive, I discover that the French government is considering the outlawing of all beards, whether male or female. It is a common suspicion in our area that the Fourth Republic will soon be taxing moustaches to increase revenue, but this proposition seems bizarre even for France. Reading on, I see that the idea is to try and ease tension by banning all overt religious symbols. There are now five million Muslims in France, and the Education minister believes making them and the thousands of Sikhs living in Paris learn to shave may be a step towards racial and religious harmony. Reflecting that politicians seem to have the same misunderstanding of human nature wherever they live and work, I look up to see one of the synchronised drinking team fall badly out of rhythm as he rapidly crosses his chest. A gust of wind rattles the doorknob, and I realise that my friend the Count of Nulleplace has arrived.

As I stand to greet him, a shadow passes the window, the

114

door swings open, and my friend appears suddenly on the threshold. I am sure that it is only coincidental that the watery sun disappears beneath a cloud to coincide with a rumble of distant thunder as the tall and gaunt figure materialises, but the Count certainly has a knack of making a dramatic entrance.

I first met Henri Charrier when we were looking for a new home in the area and had taken shelter in a remote bar during a thunderstorm. Rather than being one of the legion of the undead he is actually a highly skilled clock-restorer, but likes to play up to the role he has been given by the more superstitious members of the community. His eyes are red-rimmed and his complexion pallid because he spends long hours under strong light staring through a magnifying glass at tiny components. He also prefers to pass the daylight hours behind the heavily-curtained windows of his home and workshop, and his insistence that his steaks be served in a pool of blood is because he is French, not Transylvanian.

Henri's ancestors were local landowners before the organisers of The Terror relieved them of their heads and properties, and I do not think for a moment that any of the villagers really believe he is a vampire. But this area of the Cotentin is renowned for its penchant for the supernatural, and the villagers obviously enjoy the game as much as Henri. As well as habitually dressing in black and scrupulously avoiding any mirrors, my friend fuels the fire by being the only Frenchman I know to declare himself averse to garlic.

When we have made our greetings and I have fetched him a drink, I ask Henri if he feels a certain chill in the air. On cue, he smiles sardonically and says he is surely the last person to ask such a question. Seeing I am serious, he shrugs and says that there has been some unease about the arrival of so many British settlers in recent times. Matters came to a head when the Englishman re-opened the bar at St Clair. Understandably, Madame is not too pleased to have the competition, and as I am her best customer she is naturally unhappy that I have been frequenting a rival bar. Her customers are also unhappy to see what they think of as a British ghetto becoming established in the midst of their community.

It is not just because the newcomers are British, Henri explains, but because they insist on being so British. Local people with houses to sell are very pleased to do business with them, as are the tradesmen and others who may benefit financially from the arrival of outsiders. What the villagers do not understand is why so many of the newcomers seem so unhappy to be in the place in which they have chosen to live. And why they make no effort to try to speak the French language and absorb at least a little of the local and national culture. I, says my friend with another indecipherable shrug, am a good example of what can be accomplished by a foreigner who adapts to living in another land. After all these years I still speak French like a Spanish cow with a speech impediment, but at least I seem to have my heart in the right place - which is of course Lower Normandy. But the villagers know that I spend my time telling people about how wonderful life is in this part of France, and believe that I have contributed to the huge increase of expatriate British. Having read my books, he knows that I have probably put more Britons off settling in this area than I have encouraged to come here, but the local people do not understand this.

With his usual impeccable manners, my friend apologises for being so blunt, but says he thinks it best I understand the situation. Feelings are running quite high, and something needs to be done. There was never any problem with foreign settlers before, but then there were so few that they were, like me, a curiosity rather than a threat. When feeling their culture is under siege, even reasonable people can become unreasonable.

Henri leaves to refill our glasses and allow me time to consider what he has said. I have heard of a degree of resentment about *l'invasion* in other parts of France, but had not thought it could happen here. In my experience, Normans are the most tolerant of people. They are also very financially astute, and in a region where until recently there were more

116

empty and unwanted houses than potential buyers, the arrival of British incomers was generally welcomed. They not only brought money into the area, but were also a constant source of entertainment with their strange ways. But, as Henri said, what was once seen as a welcome influx of new blood and money could now be perceived as a threat.

When he returns, I tell the Count of Nulleplace I have had an idea. I have gained much from my time in this part of Normandy, and perhaps I can now give a little back. I will be pleased to act as a go-between and try to persuade the British settlers in the area to take more of an interest in French-and particularly Norman-culture. I will also try to help them become more interested in the *lingua franca*. In fact, I have already thought of an initial project which will enable both local bars to live up to their names, and also benefit their customers and owners.

My proposal is for a weekly get-together, held alternately at the two bars. The regulars at each venue could take it in turns to be hosts, with a language lesson for the visitors followed by a friendly competition. After the English lesson at the Entente Cordiale the visitors could take on their hosts at darts, and a friendly *boules* match could be held the following week at the Bar des Amis. Each evening could end with an informal dinner, with the menu exampling favourite dishes of the host nation. As the originator of the scheme I will not only be happy to organise the project, but also to play the role of teacher at the language lessons in each bar. Warming to my theme, I say that we could also think about twinning the two bars. Just as the inhabitants of towns on each side of the Channel foster goodwill with the *jumelage* system, we could do the same with the Entente Cordial and Bar des Amis. When the weekly exchange visits were working smoothly, we could even suggest that Madame Poelet and Simon swap places and run each other's bars for one weekend a month.

Feeling rather smug at having solved the problem of integration in such a short time, I take a long draught of my beer and wait for my friend's response. After a contemplative look at his glass, Henri says he thinks my proposal a splendid idea, but he has some minor reservations. Apart from the fact (as I should know) that there is no such thing as a friendly boules match, he is not sure that too many of the customers at this bar would be enthusiastic about learning English at their time of life. He is absolutely certain that they will not be interested in trying English food. Also, he does not think it a good idea that I should be the teacher for the French lessons. With all respect, he adds, it is difficult enough for the local people to understand what I am trying to say, and the idea of dozens of people mangling their language as I do could actually have the reverse effect to that intended. With my agreement, he will be the *professeur* at the French lessons. I would perhaps be better suited to spreading the word and enrolling members. When and if the customers of the Bar des Amis make their visit to the English pub, he can also think of no finer person than me to look after arrangements for, as he believes we English like to say, the beer and skittles.

*   *   *   *   *

I have encountered hostility for the second time today, and this time it has come from an unexpected quarter. My wife is not at all keen on my ideas for becoming the goodwill ambassador for the British community, and even less so with regards to my scheme to personally oversee and work on the conversion of the stable block.

When I told her about my plans for forging a better relationship between the locals and the newcomers, she forecast that the result would make the Hundred Years War look like a skirmish. When I said I intended doing most of the work on the stable block myself and hiring in skilled labour when necessary, she laughed entirely without humour and said

118

the idea was to convert the old building into comfortable bedrooms, not a death trap. Unless we intended running special courses for trainee Health and Safety inspectors or the more foolhardy members of dangerous sports societies, the job must be done properly. When I said I had asked a friend to recommend some local craftsmen, she reminded me of all the highly recommended craftsmen we had employed over the years, and what the results had been. After fifteen years at our former home, I had managed to make the mill cottage a damper and more uncomfortable place than it had been for the previous two hundred years. This time she will be taking control of the conversion project. My job will be to do the labouring work in the mornings and pretend to write my new book in the afternoons.

Retreating to my writing shed to sulk and appear to make a start on the record of our time at Le Marais, I wonder why my wife is in such a bad mood, then realise that she is as worried as I am about our future. We really are drinking in the Last Chance saloon, and if we do not succeed at making our new home pay its way we shall soon have nowhere to live.

In the past, I have often thought about the attractions of taking to the road or river to travel around France without the responsibilities of debts and a property to maintain. As I get older, though, the appeal of being such a free spirit diminishes. Most people need a place to call home, and unless all goes well with our latest venture we could be without a place to hang our hats or hearts.

*   *   *   *   *

My muse is still elsewhere, so I have given up for another day. Donella says my claim to be stricken with writer's block is just an excuse for not working, but she does not understand how depressing it is to sit and wait for inspiration to come. The

119

French call the problem *le syndrome de la page blanche,* and the pages of my notebook seem intent on remaining totally white.

Turning to an old copy of *The Daily Telegraph* I smuggled into the shed, my spirits are lifted by the news that my wife has every chance of living to a great age. According to the report, an American professor has spent years of intense research in coming up with the astonishing revelation that the way we live our lives can determine how long they are. He has even constructed a formula and series of equations to allow people to work out their life expectancy. Basically, the final figure is reached by starting with the average span of seventy nine years, then adding or subtracting years depending on various aspects of character and lifestyle. Three years may be added for having a sense of humour, and taking regular exercise and maintaining a healthy diet also add to the total. Smokers must deduct eight years from their tally, while being in love adds a bonus of seven years. Best news of all is that keeping what the professor calls an active pet adds two years to life expectancy, and a passive pet will earn its owner an extra twelve months.

Putting one of the blank pages in my notebook to good use, I calculate that, despite being married to me, the extra years won by owning a dog, a cat, four chickens, a dozen ducks and geese and at least two hundred very active gold fish entitles my wife to expect a lifespan of a little over three centuries. I then apply the parameters to myself and find that, without claiming co-ownership of our pets, the results indicate that I should have died in 1989.

I think about telling my wife about the test, but decide against it. She would only use the life-expanding qualities of pet animals as an excuse to buy even more, and would anyway be devastated at the thought of - if the predictions of my likely lifespan are anywhere near correct - so many long and lonely years without me at her side.

*   *   *   *   *

The fox regards me steadily, and hardly flinches when I lift my arm and throw a rasher of bacon across the river between us. My aim is bad, and the slice falls short and sinks beneath the surface. I will retrieve it later, as it is best back bacon and will taste no worse for its ducking. I try again and the rasher lands safely in the grass alongside the vixen. She takes it quickly and disappears into her run through the bramble patch. It is most likely that she is heading for a place of safety before eating, but I prefer to think she is taking the bacon home to share with her family.

It is now a week since we first met and I think the pretty vixen is beginning to trust me. I have not tried to cross the river and do not want to risk scaring her off, but I am sure she now recognises and even relies on me. I have been coming here every day at this time, and today she was waiting at the entrance to her run. Though dusk is the best time to see foxes, it is a common misconception that they are purely nocturnal. I do not know how well they can see in the dark, but I want her to know it is me approaching. A favoured way of killing a fox in this area is to catch it in a torch beam then shoot it while it sits mesmerised by the light. In those circumstances, even the typical Cotentinese hunter cannot miss his mark.

I roll a cigarette and think about why I have not told Donella about the fox and our nightly trysts. I also feel guilty about leaving Milly at home, but this is something I need to do alone. My wife would be delighted to know that I was feeding a wild animal and my dog would pose no threat, but I suppose a man needs to have something which he does completely on his own. With some it will be building a matchstick model of the *Titanic* in the garden shed, but I do not have the inclination or patience. For me, it is very special to get to know and hopefully befriend this beautiful and clever creature.

Wading into the river to fish out the bacon, I take the opportunity to pick a bunch of wild watercress. It grows profusely in the marshlands, but is one of the few free foods that local people seem to ignore. A few leaves of the cultivated variety served as an exotic dressing in an expensive restaurant would be prized by fashionable diners, but in this area the peppery-tasting leaves are seen as weeds.

A shadow falls across the water, and I look up to see a pair of brown rubber boots. They encase the feet of the guardian of the marsh, and straightening up I note that Albert is also wearing his official hat. I am further disconcerted to see that he is frowning as he looks at my bunch of watercress with both eyes, so an official reprimand seems inevitable.

I clamber on to the bank and stand like a schoolboy caught scrumping apples, but find I have misread the situation. After nodding with satisfaction, he adjusts the peak of his hat and says how pleased he is to see that I am taking my responsibilities as a new resident so seriously. I look blankly at him until he says that this section of the river will flow more swiftly and cleanly now that I have pulled up so much of the *mauvaise herbe*. He has seen me coming to this spot every day, and noticed how much of the weed I have removed. But he is also puzzled as to why I am holding a wet slice of bacon.

I think for a moment about telling him that it is an old Anglo-Saxon custom to give a gift to the river in return for its bounty, but rather lamely explain that the rasher dropped out of my pocket while I was doing the weeding. One of his eyes swivels skywards as he probably considers asking why I would choose to walk around with a slice of bacon in my pocket, but contents himself with a minimalist shrug.

I ask him if he would like a cigarette, and an obvious inner struggle takes place before he nods and takes off his hat. We settle down on the river bank, and before taking my pouch he reaches into the pocket on the front of his overalls and brings out a small bottle. It contains, he says with a disconcerting wink of his errant eye, his dinner. I take and open the bottle, and the sharp tang of home-brew apple brandy mingles with the scent of the watercress and burning tobacco.

We exchange shrugs, then take our ease on the bank and sit in silent companionship as dusk falls on the sweetly flowing river and across the great reaches of the marshlands.

* * * * *

In the next hour my friend and I smoke three cigarettes each and empty the bottle, and I am reminded of why so many rural Frenchmen prefer to do their drinking in the countryside rather than under a roof.

After a minor disagreement over the identification and relative locations of Venus and Orion, Albert told me about himself and his life. Rather than the diatribe about his famous ancestor which I heard at our first meeting, he talked simply yet eloquently about his love of the marshlands and the changes of the landscape through the seasons. His work at the rubbish tip is his job, but his work here is his vocation. He lives alone in a rented cottage in the village, envies me for having the *marais* as my garden, but feels that I understand and appreciate the privilege. Someone was anyway going to buy the big house at a price that a local person would or could not pay, and it is better that I own it rather than a real foreigner such as a rich Parisian who would use it only as a weekend cottage. If I wish to learn more about the *marais*, I may accompany him on his rounds from time to time. He has heard that I am attempting to bring the English settlers into the community, and though he thinks I am wasting my time, admires me for trying.

I responded by telling him that I would be honoured to be his pupil and that I hope we may become friends. At this he gave an acquiescent little shrug, and we are now saying our goodnights.

As I turn and walk towards the distant lights of our new home, Albert calls after me to ask if I have seen the hole in the bramble patch on the other side of the river. It is an obvious fox run, so he hopes that I will lock my chickens safely in their coop tonight. I thank him for the information, and say that I will take care not to give the fox a free dinner. Taking his hat from his pocket, he gives a wry smile and says that one cannot blame the vixen for wanting to feed herself and her family, especially with winter coming on. Like every other creature on the marais, she is his responsibility. He knows that most people would kill a fox on sight and that he, as a member of the local hunting society, should report any evidence of a run. But in this case, he thinks it should remain our secret. As he puts on his hat, he says it is remarkable what a hungry fox will eat to survive. Once he left an old leather boot out at night, and it was gone the next morning.

Of course, any fox would appreciate something more edible, and he would imagine that, even if it came from Britain, the occasional slice of bacon would be a gift from heaven for a French fox.

I cannot look at the leaf of a tree
without being overwhelmed by the universe.

Victor Hugo

9

The Devil has relieved his bladder, so the marsh blackberries are beyond even my wife's redemptive skills. The weathermen are forecasting that we are in for the hardest winter in living memory, and people live to a great age in this part of France.

There was a small scandal recently when it was revealed that any official weather prediction for more than three days ahead has no more than a fifty-fifty chance of being accurate. During a television debate and when badgered by an interviewer as to how he could be so sure a severe winter lies ahead, the senior forecaster for the region lost his patience and asked if the reporter had seen the size and abundance of the wild fruit this autumn. Also, any person with an interest in the weather would have heard how thick the onion skins were this season, which is a certain indicator of hard times ahead.

It is good to know that even nowadays folklore is sometimes seen as more reliable than the most modern technology.

When I went to feed my fox and collect the last of the wild watercress this morning, each footstep cracked like a distant pistol shot. Like a sponge, the rich earth of the plain has soaked up the heavy rains of the past month and the surface is covered with a fragile membrane of ice. When the thaw sets in and the earth can absorb no more downpours, we shall have a vast lake on our doorstep. But for now it is more like a giant's skating rink. Except for the hardiest breeds and those horses whose ownership is disputed, all farm animals have been taken to their winter quarters and only the hunters can be seen moving furtively around the killing grounds beyond our balcony.

While it is quiet on the ground, the steel-grey sky above the marshland is busy with travellers arriving or calling by on their way to more exotic destinations. The last swallows are leaving us, and it is fascinating to realise that those who survive their long journey will return to the same beam in the same building where they raised this summer's family. Also on the wing are house martins, chiffchaffs and blackcap warblers, all following the sun and drifting south, while the sweet-sharp call of redwings and fieldfares pierce the night as they arrive from the arctic to take over the fields and hedgerows. Then come the ragged skeins of ghostly white-fronted grey geese and groups of pintails, teal and widgeon ducks. It is glorious to stand on the stone balcony and speed this great aerial display on its way - and try to warn our fleeting visitors of the danger lurking below under bush and camouflage netting. Even in rural France there are laws to protect most of the birds passing overhead, but a lustful hunter with his finger on the trigger is not a man to pay scrupulous attention to any petty regulations imposed by men in suits and far away from nature's call.

Although the sudden descent into winter has brought such transports of delight, it will not be a good time to start building work. But we must have our bed and breakfast accommodation ready for Christmas, and the dramatic change in the weather has also given me some ideas for attracting extra visitors to our new venture.

As it seems we are to see the first snow in the region for a decade, I have suggested that we offer a special seasonal package holiday for Britons with young children. I could dress

126

up as Father Christmas and take the children on rides around the *marais*, with a home-made sleigh pulled by Mr Querville's giant dog. With a pair of false antlers, Zakur could pass as a fully-grown reindeer and we might even be able to persuade our neighbour to wear a pointed hat and pose as my elfin helper. In her current mood, Donella predictably poured cold water on my idea and said that Mr Querville would frighten the children, I would inevitably manage to stray off the track and sink the sledge, and we would be sued by the parents for the trauma they and their broods had suffered.

As well as refusing to take seriously any of my proposals for marketing Le Marais as a holiday destination with a difference, Donella has also barred me from interviewing any of the craftsmen who have responded to her advertisement in the local paper. While she auditions them, I have been instructed to go to town to locate some second-hand beds for the new bedrooms. I am only to look at what is on offer and report back to her, and have anyway been given no money in case I return from the bric-a-brac store at Sourciéville with an elephant's foot umbrella stand rather than a selection of minimally-used divans. When I objected to being sent on my mission with empty pockets, my wife reminded me of the story of *Jack and the Beanstalk* and how the feckless son gives away the family cow for a handful of beans. When I reminded her that the beans grew into a magic beanstalk that led to a huge bag of gold, she pointed out that though our life sometimes seemed to be an eternal pantomime, happy endings really only happen in fairy tales.

*   *   *   *   *

Frail bumper confronting massive mudguard, the tiny Deux Cheveaux squares up to the giant earthmover as David to Goliath. The owner of the car is standing by the bonnet and the flailing of his arms makes it look as if he is fending off an attack by a squadron of imaginary hornets. The driver of the earthmover is sitting calmly in the cab, safe and superior in his elevated stronghold. Now and then, he leans out of the window and shrugs unconcernedly. In Britain, this could be the prelude to violence; here it is just part of a game, and both the men would be astonished if the other did more than make extravagant gestures.

Exhausting his arm-waving repertoire, the 2CV driver squeezes back into his seat and the bonnet rears as he crunches the machine into gear. I lay mental odds on what will happen next, and swiftly win my bet. Rather than reverse and give best to the behemoth and its driver, the man has obviously decided to make a grand if doomed gesture. Accordingly, the Citroën lurches forward and crashes into the steel girder which runs across the front of the earthmover, and a trio of labourers in fluorescent jackets and hard hats abandon their posts and hurry over to enjoy the encounter. The man who is supposed to be directing traffic through the road works lays down his stop-go sign and joins them, ensuring further chaos.

I am in no hurry, so settle down with as much anticipation as the rest of the drivers in the growing queue. I shall only be browsing at the second-hand furniture store at Sourciéville, and however pressing the business of the other travellers, the drama about to unfold will surely make our wait worthwhile. *Caleçon* is French for underpants, and for some reason *une caleçonnade* is a roadshow with risqué elements. By all appearances, we are due for a very promising *spectacle de boulevard*.

Having locked metaphorical horns with its towering opponent, the Citroën is predictably making no forward progress, and the two iron horses beneath the bonnet whinny with frustration as wheels spin impotently and smoke issues from both ends of the vehicle. In an equally fruitless gesture, the driver and his large lady passenger begin to bounce up and down in their seats to gain traction, while the spectators urge them on with additional tips on how to achieve the palpably impossible.

Eventually and to the obvious disappointment of the onlookers, the driver accepts the inevitable. With another vicious crunching of gears, the Deux Chevaux limps backwards to allow minimum clearance, then buzzes alongside and past the earthmover to the unreserved applause of the spectators. As a parting shot, the driver thrusts a hand out of the window to make an offensive gesture at his opponent and then a regally gracious acknowledgement to his supporters. The encounter has cost the car and its owner a mangled bumper, a few millimetres of tyre tread and several hundred miles of engine wear. But he has made his point and won the admiration of his audience. As with so many aspects of French life, winning a battle is not always as important as the style with which it is fought.

The *cinema* over, the workers return to their tools and the director of traffic picks up his sign. About to give the go-ahead to the line facing the queue in which I am sitting, he sees that it is headed by a car with British licence plates and changes his mind. Spinning the signboard round, he waves the car in front of me through, and I nod sympathetically at the driver of the Range Rover as I pass by. He has obviously not enjoyed the entertainment or the delay, and scowls in return at what he thinks is a smug foreigner.

Reflecting on the incidental benefits of driving a locally licensed and thus number-plated car, I navigate the road works which have been causing daily chaos on the outskirts of Sourciéville for the past week. Until then, this back route into town passed through a peaceful area of countryside with no more than a handful of houses dotted alongside one of the three rivers meandering towards the port. Now, a commercial park is being built here and the landscape has been laid to waste. The warehouses and superstores will offer cut-price household goods and groceries, but the cost will be borne by the small shops in the market square. In aesthetic terms, the cost will also be borne by the once-timeless beauty of this small part of the peninsula. Progress is inevitable and sometimes desirable, but it comes in this case with a heavy hand and high price.

Slowing down at the start of another contra-flow, I look out across the scarred terrain and see an immaculately maintained cottage standing alone amongst the desolation. By the door, an old man in a grey suit and a collarless white shirt stands watching as an earthmover gobbles up a mouthful of rich topsoil. Amongst the churned-up earth I can see a sprinkling of bamboo canes and shreds of foliage, so assume the machine is eating what was once a vegetable patch. The old man is regarding the machine and its activities impassively, and I am reminded of a wartime photograph of a family watching from a doorway as a line of German troops marched through their village. They too were looking at something which they were powerless to prevent.

But sometimes things are not as we see them, and perhaps the old man is to be relocated to a comfortable new home in the town and does not object to the loss. It may be that he has been paid a previously unimaginable sum for his cottage, or that he is its tenant and not owner. Perhaps he does not even live in the house, and is merely resting during a long walk into town. If I could, I would stop and ask him what his situation is and how he feels about what is happening. If he is walking to Sourciéville, I could offer him a lift and find out about his life and thoughts.

As it is, the signboard swings and I must move on. Looking back at the scene, I see there is a washing line beside the cottage and from it hang at least a dozen old shoes and boots. Curiously, none of them makes up a pair, and I wonder what their singularity signifies. It appears that the old man has two legs, so if he is the owner it is possible that he is collecting them to throw at the bulldozers when they arrive to tear down his home. Perhaps, being a Norman, he is hoping that a disabled driver with the right foot size will stop and make him an offer for his entire stock.

An impatient blast from behind reminds me of my duty,

and I drive away from another small but intriguing mystery which must remain eternally unsolved.

*   *   *   *   *

As it is for some people with pubs or cake or betting shops, I find it hard to pass a *brocante*.

These peculiarly French second-hand stores are also museums registering the changing times and fashions, and I can spend hours wandering through the jumble of classic period furniture, disassembled self-assembly kitchens and broken electrical goods. In this part of France, it is considered almost a mortal sin to throw anything away that might be of some conceivable use to someone else, especially if they might be prepared to pay for it. Though many Normans like to live up to their reputation for frugality, I do not think that our country people are particularly mean. It is more that older people here like to live within the social framework of their time. In their youth, conspicuous consumption and disposal was not seen as an admirable way of life.

The *brocante* at Sourciéville is the only trading post of its kind in the area, so the turnover of the most popular items is brisk. It pays to be an early bird at the winningly-named *Ile de Trésor* if you are in search of a bargain.

The cavernous treasurehouse is owned and run by a sharp-witted and even sharper-tongued lady who is alleged to have once been the Madam at a house of pleasure in the dockland area of Marseilles. If this is true, her former profession, home town and temperament have equipped her ideally for what she does now.

Each day at dawn, scores of people arrive with something to sell and to ask the proprietor to grant it floor or shelf space. The would-be vendors will naturally think their dysfunctional television set or three-legged coffee table a valuable commodity

131

and certain seller, but Madame will not always agree. If she does, the first hurdle will have been passed, but then will come the sometimes bruising business of deciding on a suitable price to put on the item. In the normal way of these affairs, Madame Jolie does not buy the goods herself, but takes a commission when they are sold. As she naturally prefers the swiftest of returns for her floor space, her idea of what any item is worth is invariably well below that of its owner.

Although Normans are said to be the hardest of bargainers, it is rare that they get the better of Madame, and she always holds the trump card. Exchanges can be more than bracing, and her glass-fronted eyrie overlooking the ground floor of the *brocante* is a popular gathering place for those who enjoy witnessing a lively debate. I have learned more interesting colloquialisms and expletives by standing at the door of Madame's office than in the most colourful of quayside taverns.

At this time of day, the deals have all taken place, the supplicants gone away happy or discontented, and Madame is now quietly keeping an eye on her stock and customers. After an exchange of greetings, I explain my mission and she escorts me on a tour of inspection. This is not so much a courtesy as a necessity, as the bedroom furniture will not be displayed in one dedicated section of the warehouse. Rather than an inefficient practice, this is a deliberate ploy, as Madame knows that there is always a chance that a customer looking for a specific item is quite likely to see something else they like while searching for it. Madame Jolie also knows that hiding an otherwise unremarkable item in an unexpected location can lend it appeal far beyond its actual worth. I also suspect that I am being given the guided tour because she has seen me in action and does not want her stock damaged as I dig for what may be buried treasure.

As we descend the stairs, I see a knot of customers gathered around what looks like a display more suited to a modern art gallery. Drawing closer, I realise that it is half a set of quality furniture. By this I do not mean half the items one would expect to find in such a collection, but actually one half of each of the pieces on show.

Nearest the aisle is an elegant *chaise longue* which is no longer as long as when it was created. Inexplicably, it has been sawn roughly in half. Beyond the truncated daybed is half a fine mahogany dining table, and propped against it are the remains of six once elegant and extremely valuable chairs. The left-hand side of a writing bureau is resting against the back wall, and beside it is an amputee buffet with a selection of quality china carefully arranged on the remnants of its shelving.

I look at Madame for guidance, and she tells me the story. The display is not the work of an inspired artist making a protest against materialism, but a betrayed husband with rage in his heart and a chainsaw to hand.

Madame Jolie explains that she was offered the vandalised furniture by a local woman who married an English solicitor she had met whilst in London. They had set up home in Sourciéville and furnished it lovingly with the best period furniture. Though their marriage had started well, she had begun to resent his week-long absences in England, and found solace in the arms of the dealer who had sold them the antique furniture. When her husband had discovered the affair and threatened to divorce her, she reminded him that although they had been married for but a short while she would be entitled to at least half the house and furniture he had paid for. As he was a foreigner, it was quite likely that she would be awarded more than half of their assets in France.

After an evening drinking with sympathetic friends in a local bar, the husband had returned with a borrowed chainsaw and said he wanted to make an immediate start on dividing their assets equally. Having attended to the lounge furniture, he had started on the rest of the house, but the blade of his saw had thankfully become jammed fast in a leg of pork while trying to cut the fridge-freezer in half.

The police arriving too late to apprehend him, her husband had disappeared into the night with a van containing his share of the furniture, and the woman had appealed to Madame Jolie for help. Although she knew that it was very unlikely anyone would want to buy such damaged goods, the shrewd owner had realised that the evidence of the broken marriage would make an eye-catching display, and people had travelled from all over the region to see and wince at the barbarous if understandable vandalism.

Madame had grown a little tired about the enquiries as to whether the items were on hire purchase, with half on deposit and the rest on completion of payment, but the tableau had been good for business. She was also pleased to report that it looked as if there might be a happy ending to the small tragedy. Impressed by the passion shown by her normally reserved British husband, the woman was trying to persuade him to return. Apart from the joy of reconciliation, there was also the possibility that his half of the desecrated furniture would come back with him, and it might be possible to re-unite the separate pieces as well as the couple. It would take a very skilled restorer to repair the damage, Madame thought, but she had heard that the woman's former lover had offered his services to mend the rift that he had originally created.

*   *   *   *   *

I have returned to Le Marais to find my wife bandaging the head of a stranger. As she secures the turban of strips of old bed linen with a safety pin, Donella introduces Mr Balourd and explains that he has just met one of our low door frames.

Standing to shake my hand, the tall and somehow awkward-looking man apologises for bleeding on our carpet and says he will make good any damage to our property the collision has caused. As he is one of the craftsmen come to estimate for the work to be done on the stable block, I take this as a good sign and nod approvingly at my wife. She returns the nod to let me know she is in favour of engaging Mr Balourd.

When I have pressed him to take another medicinal glass of *calva*, he resumes his seat and says that he would be most happy to help with our project. He has inspected the stable block, talked with my wife about what is needed, and sees no problem. When I ask what his range of skills are, he blows out his cheeks and stretches out his arms, knocking his glass on to the stone flagged floor. While my wife sweeps up, he apologises profusely and promises to deduct the cost of the glass from his bill, then explains that, unusually in rural France, he is a general builder and would sub-contract any specialist craftsmen needed for the project. He is free to start immediately, and will require no advance payment. Rather than an estimate for the job, he would prefer to work for a set day rate. If given the contract, he will be on duty precisely eight hours a day, not including his lunch and refreshment breaks, and will drive a hard bargain on our behalf with any additional tradesmen we will need.

Having learned the cost of his daily attendance, I say we will be pleased to engage Mr Balourd, and would like him to start work as soon as possible. I will be available to help with the heavy work each morning, and will also be able to discuss any aspects of decor or technical matters that arise during the project.

The deal having been struck, I walk our newly-appointed builder to the gate. As we stroll across the yard I cannot help but notice that he has a finger missing from one hand, seems to rely on his right leg and that the other appears to be squeaking. Seeing my look, he says that he lost the leg and a finger in separate building site accidents but the injuries will not affect his ability to do his work. Thinking of my recent correspondence about the singular-limbed bricklayer, I shake his hand then pat his other arm while bidding him goodnight and am pleased to feel pliant flesh rather than unyielding plastic.

As he waves and limps to his car, I lean on the gate and consider how our luck seems to be changing. Though not as cheap as the one-armed brickie, Mr Balourd obviously makes an allowance for his missing parts when setting a rate for his services. More importantly, he is my wife's choice of contractor, so if anything goes wrong during the work on the stable block it will not be all my fault.

*   *   *   *   *

At The Good Intent, Simon is still polishing his pump handles and the red-faced man is still complaining about *la vie Francaise*.

Since our first meeting, I have learned that his name is Conan, and that before retiring he was a librarian. It is interesting that he dislikes everything about a country where the diminutive of his Christian name is a very rude word, and one that describes exactly what most local people might think of their ungrateful lodger.

Now that I have got to know Conan better, I do not think he is a bad man. He is just lonely and alone in a foreign country, and needs something and someone else to blame for his mistake in choosing to live abroad. I think he would be as miserable in Spain or Italy as he is here, and if he had stayed at home he would probably be sitting in a pub complaining about everything in modern Britain.

We have come to the British bar for dinner, and the official excuse is to mark the engagement of Mr Balourd to carry out the work on our stable block. Although I suggested having a meal here as a way of making a small contribution to Simon and Saskia's profits, I have an ulterior motive. The visit will enable me to launch my self-appointed role as goodwill ambassador between the two communities, and while we are here I shall hopefully be able to enrol some members for the French lessons course.

Pretending to listen to the rantings of Conan the Librarian while ordering our drinks and food, I ask Simon if his wife is on duty in the kitchen but he does not reply.

Bemused when he hands me a large wooden mixing spoon with a number printed on the bowl, I ask him what it is for. When he says I must keep it with me, I ask him if he means for life. With a taut expression, he explains that the number tallies with our order, and I should place it in the special holder attached to the table at which we decide to sit. This will let the person serving our meal know where it should be delivered.

I look around the bar before pointing out that, apart from Conan, we are the only customers in the bar. Also, as he has just taken our order and will assumedly be the person serving it, he is unlikely to have a problem in uniting us with our steak and kidney puddings.

Our host stares at me for a lip-quivering moment then asks in a strained voice if I think I could run his business better than him. If so, he says, I am welcome to try. He then snatches the spoon from my hand and barges through the swing door to the kitchen.

I look at my wife and shrug, and she glares at me as we walk over to a corner table. When I ask her what is wrong, she says that I have once again proved myself to be as sensitive as a house-brick. It is obvious that the business is not doing well and that Simon is under a lot of pressure. The last thing he will need at the moment is somebody like me trying to be clever at his expense. Even I must have noticed that his wife has not been seen in the bar for almost a month, and it is likely that she has left him.

I open my mouth to ask why making a joke about a wooden spoon was such an insensitive thing to do, but decide it will be safer to let the matter lie. Sometimes and even after so many years of marriage I find it very hard to understand my wife, let alone other people.

*   *   *   *   *

We have eaten, the bar is comfortably full, and Donella is in a better mood. We have also talked about our plans for the stable block, and made some rough calculations of projected overheads and income. I said that we should charge a premium rate for B&B and make capital of our guests being able to stay at the home of a fairly famous author. My wife disagrees and thinks we should keep the prices low, and also keep quiet about my presence at Le Marais. If the potential customers have not heard of me, it will make no difference to whether they choose to stay with us. If they have read my books it may well put them off coming.

I have also made encouraging progress with my mission to bring the two communities together, and half a dozen customers have promised to come to the first language session at the Bar des Amis. Eric likes the idea of showing off his virtual dog to the locals and agrees that it might be useful to learn a few words of command in French. Surprisingly, Conan has agreed to attend, but only after I told him there would be free drinks following the lesson.

I have invited all our students to join us so we may get to know each other a little better. To put them at their ease, I suggested that we formally introduce ourselves, and the first speaker was Dafyd. He is a nervous-looking man with a wispy beard and bottle-bottom glasses who is a former teacher specialising in his native language of Welsh. He speaks French very well, and I suspect he is coming to the classes so he can impress us with his linguistic ability and encyclopaedic knowledge of little-known facts. He is one of those people who delights in collecting information which most people would not be aware of, and many would not wish to know. After introducing himself, he said he had spent the day researching and collating relative statistics for a book he is hoping to have published. An interesting example of his findings is the fact that there are 270 words in the Ten Commandments, 2,700 words in the United States Declaration of Independence, and 270,000 words in the EU Regulations for the import and export of duck eggs. Somehow, the last statistic does not surprise me. When he moved on to reveal that human beings have fewer genes than the average garden weed and only twice as many as the common fruit fly, I thanked him for the information and made a mental note to suggest we form a pub quiz team and challenge the Bar des Amis to a friendly encounter.

The next member of our circle to introduce herself was a lady who I think would be the odds-on favourite for next year's Flaming Curtains Absinthe Challenge. Her name is Pat, and she is married to a man who would probably be her biggest rival for the winner's cup. Pat and Ron are ex-publicans and make no secret that they are economic migrants. It was not, however, the price of property that attracted them to the idea of living in France, but the price of drink and cigarettes. After retiring from their busy pub in the Midlands and realising that the weekly bill at their local was exceeding the combined cost of every other overhead, they had started to make regular runs to France to stock up on duty-free alcohol and cigarettes. When some busybody representing the Customs and Excise refused to believe that the sheer volume of their monthly import was purely for personal use and confiscated their car, the couple decided to move nearer to their source of supply. Now, they are very happy in their small cottage on the outskirts of a nearby village and feel they have integrated well with the local community.

As Pat explained, they have been given every assistance by the mayor of their commune, though were recently embarrassed by the arrival of a facility which has apparently been laid on for their exclusive use.

In their first month as members of the commune, the couple would make weekly visits after dark to distribute their empties at a number of bottle banks in the area. Though they normally did not try to hide their enjoyment of a regular intake of wine and spirits, they did not want to give the wrong impression to their neighbours. Last week, they had been woken at dawn by the noise of a lorry outside their bedroom window and looked out to see a large and obviously new bottle bank being lowered into place on a patch of waste ground beside their house. Now, they are unsure whether it was due to be installed there anyway, or is an acknowledgement by the commune of their consumption rate and intended for their personal use.

Making up our collection of British students is someone who says she is an avid fan of mine. Veronica is a tall and very generously-built blonde lady of middle years. As the French would say, she has plenty of meat on her bones, and has obviously seen much of life. She clearly has a liking for voluminous, flowing and yet revealing garments, and as she swayed across the busy room to join our table I was put in mind of a galleon in full sail beating its way through a choppy sea.

When Donella had gone to buy a round of drinks, Veronica moved her chair closer to mine, leaned forward and said she had read every word I have written. She thinks I write very well, but that my books will only become best-sellers if I sex them up a bit. Unable to stop myself from staring into the depths of her billowing cleavage, I said the first thing that came into my head and asked if she meant my work should be sexed-up in the same way as the documents about the mythical weapons of mass destruction in Iraq. She then gave a throaty laugh which made large areas of her superstructure wobble most disconcertingly, and said she was sure I knew what she was talking about and would be happy to help me with any research I might want to undertake.

To change the subject, I asked her if she had a husband, and she replied that he had gone back to England to re-charge his batteries. When I said I would have thought the pace of life in this area more relaxing than on the other side of the Channel, she laughed again and said that he had gone back to England to re-charge the batteries in the pacemaker he needs to maintain the rhythm of his heart. Her husband's local doctor was puzzled, she said while scratching the top of one of her sheer black nylon stockings with a blood-red fingernail, that the batteries became flattened at a much quicker rate than normal.

Our conversation was cut short by the return of my wife, who had somehow forgotten Veronica's drink. Unusually, Donella did not apologise or even offer to go and buy it, and when I did, she gave me the same sort of look as during the wooden spoon incident.

So, our French language class is an interestingly mixed crowd, and I am looking forward to helping forge better relationships between the two communities and with our fellow settlers. Before we left, Veronica slipped a scrap of paper into my hand and suggested I give her a call if I was free in the next few days to give her some advance French lessons at her home. As she kissed my cheek and pressed her awesome frontage against my body-warmer, I said that I would be very busy with the work on our stable block in the mornings and my new book in the afternoons, but would bear in mind what she had said about sexing-up my work.

I do not think a racier approach would help sell more of my books, but believe Veronica was only trying to be helpful. One thing is for sure, and that is whenever I look at her imposing frontage I will find it difficult not to think about weapons of mass destruction.

Exactitude is not Truth.

Henri Matisse

10

The days grow shorter, the air clearer, and there is an almost luminescent quality to the great plain on our doorstep. Yesterday I sat and watched a man working on a roof in a hamlet at least a mile away. Appearing to over-reach while replacing a ridge tile, he stumbled, slid down the steep pitch of the roof and disappeared. I could not see how far he fell or how hard he landed, but he did not reappear again, so I phoned Albert Poubelle, who said he would drive by the house and see what had happened. If my description of the man and the location of the house is accurate, it is almost certain that the victim is a renowned toper and will have come to no harm. It is, as the guardian of the *marais* says, remarkable how a skinful of booze can often be better than a parachute when it comes to breaking a fall.

At the moment I am sitting on the balcony and cleaning fox droppings from the sole of my boot. It is my left boot, and according to my neighbour, this is a lucky omen in France. As he has dozens of dogs on his premises, I suppose Mr Querville would consider himself lucky to have such a problem with only one foot at a time. If the culprit were his giant Newfoundland, I suspect he would be up to his knee of

143

whichever leg was involved.

Apart from this convenient superstition, the rural French tend to accept the waste product of animals as a part of the landscape. Last summer, one of the main attractions at our village fete was based on the bowel motions of a cow. A field had been marked off in metre-wide squares, and before the animal was shooed in, a book was run on the square in which she would make her first deposit. My prediction was hopelessly inaccurate, and there was some ill-feeling when the person who scooped the cash prize was revealed as the owner of the cow. One of the gamblers made an official protest that the man had an unfair advantage as he would know the movements and motions of his animal. There were even allegations that the farmer had set up a grid of baling twine in one of his own field weeks before the event, and trained his cow to do its business in a particular spot.

*   *   *   *   *

Donella is at a meeting with our new bank manager, and work has begun on the accommodation centre. Or rather, work will begin when I have resolved the pigeon situation.

Mr Balourd arrived at the exact time promised, and is obviously a conscientious worker. As we are paying him by the hour, I hope he will not prove too conscientious. He seems unusually fastidious, and the only craftsman I have met who washes his hands before starting work. He also wears a worn but clean and neat suit and tie beneath his overalls. These characteristics sit oddly with his extreme cackhandedness, or have perhaps developed because of them. He is probably so deliberate in his actions to try and keep injuries to the minimum, and wearing the suit means he will not have to change from his working clothes to visit the doctor when he has one of his regular accidents.

After checking and laying out his tools like a surgeon about to undertake a demanding operation, he asked me to walk around the stable block with him so we could talk through the first stage of operations. Although I thought I had blocked up all pigeon-sized holes in the roof and walls of the old building, we got no further than a few steps inside before the bombardment started. Retreating to the kitchen, we wiped each other down and took a reviving glass of cider while discussing how best to rid the stable block of the squatters.

Mr Balourd said it would be a matter of moments for him to fetch his shotgun from home, but I explained that Donella would not approve. I did not say that letting him loose with a twelve bore in a confined space would not only be extremely dangerous but the damage caused could make the reconstruction work much more expensive. I also vetoed the idea of poison because of my wife's sensibilities. Eventually, we agreed that I would spend the rest of the day evicting the pigeons and boarding-up any other points of entry. Mr Balourd would go home for a bath, and be ready to make a fresh start in the morning.

*   *   *   *   *

Round one to the pigeons, and I am sure my neighbour is now convinced I am quite mad.

My first job being to get the messy birds out of the stable block, I tried some energetic shouting and waving but this had no effect other than causing a renewed hail of droppings. Remembering the effect music can have on animals, I took my CD player into the stables and tried a selection of tunes played at very high volume. Rather than frighten the squatters off, my choice of *Iolanthe* followed by *The Birdie Song* merely brought about a spate of contented cooing from the rafters.

It was as I stood beneath an umbrella shouting and

throwing stones at the rafters that Mr Querville appeared and asked me if I was feeling well. He said that he had heard the noise and screaming so had come to see if I was having a fit. When I said I was preparing the building for some restoration work, he said that unless it was a traditional ceremony in my country, throwing stones at and abusing a building did not seem a good way to make a start on restoring it. On a more practical note, he had heard I was going to try and persuade British holidaymakers to pay huge sums of money to sleep in a stable, so perhaps I would send him any spare customers as he could always find a space for them in his kennel block.

When I explained the problem with the unwanted birds, he sucked his teeth, shook his head and asked if there was not an expression in my language which referred to setting a cat amongst pigeons. Rather than admit I had not thought of such a simple solution, I said that my wife was, like him, an animal lover and would not want to see the birds harmed. After saying that pigeons did not count as animals, he said that if I wanted to frighten them off without causing any physical harm, I could just show them a photograph of my devil-cat.

*   *   *   *   *

Round two to the pigeons.

When Mr Querville had gone, I lured Lupin into the stable block and shut the door. After a frenetic burst of fluttering screeching and yowling, all was silent and I entered to find the pigeons fled and Lupin sitting on the mud floor with his mouth full of feathers. Having boarded up a broken window pane and replaced several missing roof tiles, I went to the house and called Mr Balourd to say that the birds had flown and he could start work tomorrow. When I returned to the stable block I was met with a mocking coo and an even more devastating bombardment from the rafters. Another visit from Lupin cleared the building in moments, but in the mêlée of feathers and droppings I could not see the birds' exit point. After conducting a fingertip search and being unable to find a single hole big enough for a pigeon to pass through, I realised that I must either dismantle the whole stable block to locate their secret passage, or find a way of permanently scaring off my unwanted tenants.

*　　　*　　　*　　　*　　　*

I believe I have found the solution to our problem, and in the process learned that the average pigeon is far from stupid. Like foxes, it seems they have acquired a bad name in relatively recent times.

The formal name for the species is European rock dove, and their ancestry goes back beyond Biblical times. Pigeons are believed to be the first birds to be domesticated, and as well as arriving at Noah's Ark with an olive branch, they are believed to have taken news of the coronation of Rameses III to the outlying regions of the Egyptian empire. As is more widely known, pigeons carried messages during World War I, and with spy cameras strapped to their breasts were also used for vital aerial reconnaissance missions. A carrier pigeon known as Gustav (or NPS 42.31066 to his owners in the Air Ministry) brought news of the success of the D-Day Landings to Britain. Though hampered by a strong headwind and cloudy conditions (pigeons navigate by the sun), Gustav crossed the Channel in just over five hours, which is a better time than a lot of modern car ferries.

They are obviously heroically-minded as well as clever creatures, as more than thirty pigeons have been awarded the animal equivalent of the VC for bravery in action. The brightest birds have even been taught to recognise the alphabet, and Darwin studied the species to help evolve his theories on evolution. Quite simply, in terms of navigational instinct, courage and memory, pigeons leave some humans standing.

During my research I also learned that they mate for life, feed their babies with milk and welcome strangers into their flocks without suspicion, which is more than can be said of many human societies. In certain circumstances, it is believed that pigeons can be harbingers of death, but I will not pass that superstition on to Mr Querville to add to his endless list of ill-omens presaged by everyday events. It is of course not their fault that pigeons make such a mess, and is another example of how we demonise any species which causes us inconvenience. Nobody would blame a tiger for eating a gazelle, but we hate pigeons simply because they, like all birds and most animals, relieve themselves where they happen to be at the time. As an old farmer sagely observed while we were watching the cow-pat competition at the summer fete, it is a good job cows don't fly or we would shoot them on sight.

As often happens when we learn more about other cultures or creatures, now that I have discovered that pigeons are neither stupid nor feckless creatures I feel myself more warmly disposed towards the squatters in the stable block. Killing them is out of the question, but even Donella would not think it a good idea to let them continue their occupation of our future accommodation centre. I am also sure any future customers would not appreciate such close contact with nature if we left the birds where they are, but I have an idea which should make everyone - including the pigeons - happy. I will build them a new and comfortable home at a safe distance from the house and outbuildings, but must first serve them with an irresistible eviction notice.

My problem now is simply how to persuade them to leave and not return, and my options seem limited. With Mr Balourd waiting to make a start, I do not have the time to make a selection of imitation hawks and owls and nail them to the rafters. Spreading a special repellent gel on perching areas is said to be effective, but can be harmful and would definitely be expensive.

Then, inspiration strikes. According to the reports I have been reading, pigeons feel uncomfortable and unbalanced when landing on the sticky gel and will abandon their favourite hang-outs to move on to firmer ground. All I need to create a harmless exclusion zone in the stable block is a step ladder, a large spatula and the contents of a few of the dozens of jars on the shelves in my wife's pantry.

*   *   *   *   *

My scheme has backfired, and we now have other unwanted guests in the stable block.

Donella returned from a shopping trip yesterday evening to find no work done on the conversion of the stable block, and Mr Querville watching in bemusement as I spread several pounds of home-made blackberry jelly on the rafters. When I explained it was a humane way of evicting the pigeons she agreed on a trial period to see if it worked, but when we entered the building this morning the birds were happily feeding on the jelly.

Worse, the sugar-rich coating has attracted other scavengers and we are now threatened with a plague of rats. Mr Querville has threatened to sue us for the danger to the health and safety of his boarders, and Mr Balourd has refused to enter the building until he is safe from attack by bird or beast. My wife has employed the expensive services of a local pest controller, and I have been barred from the stable block. Providing all goes well with the rat catcher and pigeon exorcist, Mr Balourd and Donella will plug all the holes tomorrow morning and work will start in the afternoon. I have been banished to my writing shed for the rest of the day, but like the pigeons, I have a secret escape hatch.

Today it is obviously the turn of the local cycling fraternity to show its paces at the *Promenade d'Anglaise*. This means the French spectators will have some home-grown bizarre behavioural patterns to savour.

The British dog-walkers are under siege as the elevated tracks around the disused quarry swarm with lycra-clad figures doing their best to make a nuisance of themselves. The exhibition of silly hats and helmets, lurid skin-tight clothing, raised bottoms and reckless behaviour is also an opportunity to study another cultural hiatus between our two races.

Britain has a growing number of velo-exhibitionists, but most people still seem to use bicycles to get to and from work or demonstrate their moral superiority. Middle-class ladies with headscarves like to pedal around country villages and glare at motorists while their husbands are driving back and forward to their jobs in the city. Young parents show off their environmentally-conscious credentials by cycling smugly up and down country lanes before bundling their fashionably-dressed children and trendy machines into giant petrol-guzzling space wagons for the journey home. In general, double standards and hypocrisy rule. But in rural France no self-respecting woman of social status and mature years would be seen dead on a bicycle, and the average cyclist does not give a fig for the ethical credibility of his mode of travel. However, bicycle road-racing is a national passion and as eagerly followed and practiced at weekends as is soccer in Britain.

Every Saturday, millions of French men dress themselves up to look like particularly foppish members of a 1970s glam-rock band and take to the roads to emulate their sporting heroes. Like locusts, they find safety and can do the most damage in numbers, and to see a host of insect-like figures racing down a hill into an unsuspecting town is to be put in mind of the onset of a Biblical plague.

Tomorrow, these two-wheeled hooligans will be ganging up on their own countrymen, but today they are enjoying the opportunity to rehearse on foreign victims. In a way, it is like a fox-hunt, with the cyclists the pack and the dog-walkers their quarry. The object of the exercise is not to actually kill or even collide with anyone, however, as this would risk damage to the rider and his machine. Rather, individuals and groups are going for the spectacular near-miss. Like Mongol horsemen, they are showing their skills with ever-more daring displays of split-second timing and control, and there is obviously much status to be gained by wreaking the maximum havoc and instilling the highest levels of rage and terror amongst their targets.

Having left several large shards of granite strategically placed along the lower track, I see a familiar figure slumped on a nearby bench and hurry over to see if he is hurt. When I greet Lonely Eric, he raises a distraught face and says he has lost his dog. It ran away when a cyclist came too close and he has been searching and calling for Scotty for an hour. Playing along, I say that I am sure the dog will return, and if not he can always invent another one. Then I realise that Eric is quite serious in his grief. Like a child or television soap-opera addict, he has persuaded himself that his imaginary companion is at the same time real and unreal. He knows Scotty is not real, but is enjoying indulging his emotions as if he were, and the self-indulgence will cost him nothing. I am reminded of the reaction to the death of Princess Diana by millions of apparently sane people, and think about telling him to pull himself together. Instead, I pat his shoulder and say I will help him look for his pet. Whether or not Eric agrees to find the unfindable, I shall visit Mr Querville when I get home and ask if he has any puppies for sale at a neighbourly price. If I force his hand, I think Eric may learn that caring only for himself is what has made him so lonely.

Eric has been reunited with his virtual pet, but I shall still go ahead with my puppy plan. After we found Scotty allegedly hiding behind a tree and he and his master had gone off for an imaginary celebration at The Good Intent, I was returning to the car when Milly's Russian admirer came bounding out of the copse. He was followed by his minder, and trailing behind was the wife of the owner of The Good Intent. Both Jonathan and Saskia looked dishevelled and flushed, but I do not think their appearance was caused by the pursuit through the undergrowth.

When he got his breath back, Jon asked how my project was going, and when I told him about the delay with the stable block conversion he said he might have a much better business proposition for me to think about. When I asked him what the proposition was, he gave a sidelong glance at Saskia and said he would tell me about it later. After a rather stilted conversation about the weather and the plague of cyclists, I said I must get back to see how work was going at Le Marais, and the couple disappeared back into the copse. I don't know if any of the marauding hordes or riders favour off-road harrying, but there could be an interesting confrontation if they do venture off the tracks and into the wood.

On my way back to the carpark, I saw the former bus driver standing with his collie dog as he looked out across the lake. Although swarms of cyclists were buzzing around him, he looked very alone. From the set of his shoulders I knew not to mention his wife, and when I asked about the pair of swans he had been feeding, he said in a flat voice that the vet had not been able to save the female. The cob had flown off from the lake yesterday, and he had watched it go.

When I stupidly said that these things happen in nature and the swan might find a new mate and be happy with her, he looked at me for the first time. His eyes were glistening and his face crumpled with grief, yet there was a sad dignity in his composure. In almost matter-of-fact tones he told me that his wife had died an hour before the swan had flown. When I had stumbled out my condolences and asked him if he would stay in France or go home, he said that his home was now here in Normandy, and he would not be leaving his wife alone in a foreign country.

Before patting him awkwardly on the shoulder and trying to think of something to say that was not the usual inanity, I wrote down our telephone number and said he might like to give me a call if he wanted some company. When I suggested we go to a local bar if he would like to drink and talk about his wife and their life together, he took the piece of paper, thanked me and said he would prefer to be on his own for a while. He had his dog to keep him company, and, of course, his memories.

As I left him standing at the water's edge, I thought about real loss and grief, and if Eric could ever be capable of such depth of real feeling. I have observed the grim irony that those people who truly love their partners often seem to lose them in tragic circumstances, while those in unhappy unions are often stuck with theirs. The meeting with the bereaved man has also made me wonder if, all things considered, Eric is better or worse off because of his insularity and consequent immunity from real sorrow.

*   *   *   *   *

The letting rooms in the stable block are no nearer to realisation, our builder is incapacitated, and according to my wife it is all my fault.

I have a theory that the owners of private ambulance services in rural France like to be proactive, and the driver of the careering vehicle which overtook me on the road to Le

153

Marais this morning was clearly doing his best to drum up fresh business. Having failed to run me off a humpback bridge, he sped away with the wailing siren sounding somehow resentful at a missed opportunity.

Rounding a bend in the lane leading to our home I saw the flashing light by the gatepost and thought for a moment that the ambulance had doubled back and was laying in wait. But in the yard, I found my wife supervising while Mr Balourd lay stoically on a stretcher as the ambulance man removed an inflatable splint from his patient's artificial leg. As the paramedic made good his mistake, Mr Balourd apologised for the inconvenience and promised to pay for the wooden ladder he had destroyed. He had found it waiting for him in the stable block and had not realised it was rotten with worm. Through gritted teeth he said he hoped that his broken leg would not take too long to heal, but would understand if we wished to engage another craftsman to continue the work.

After waving him off and clearing up the debris, my wife and I talked about the situation and decided we will have to look for someone to replace Mr Balourd for the time being. When he is fully recovered, he can help with the finishing-off work. We are now badly behind schedule, and the bank will not wait for its repayments until we have some paying guests.

I suggested that we could delay the conversion of the stable block and use the money from the building loan to pay off the monthly installments on our mortgage, but my wife retorted that borrowing from Peter to pay Paul was exactly how we lost La Puce. When I reminded her that I had originally suggested I carry out the work on the stable block, she gave a hollow laugh and said I had already caused enough damage with my pigeon-removal scheme. And it was I who had left the worm-eaten wooden ladder for Mr Balourd to find. We were lucky he was not suing us, and the best thing I could do would be to get on with my writing. By the time my new book is finished, and the way things are going, she added rather tartly, I will certainly not be short of material.

We are assembled at the Bar des Amis, and there is a full house for the start of our French language course. All the students have kept their promises to attend, and most of the regular customers are here. I think the locals have come out of curiosity, but if I can encourage them to take part in the lessons I believe we may be able to start a dialogue between the two camps and their very different cultures. The evening did not get off to a good start when Veronica sat opposite the synchronised drinking team and put them off by constantly adjusting the swooping neckline of her sweater, but perhaps they will regain their rhythm when they become used to the size of her enormous bosoms.

Within our group, the retired British publicans are in obvious good spirit and were starting on their second bottle of house red as I arrived. When I asked if they had something special to celebrate, Pat told me about an article in a British newspaper which had persuaded them to lead a healthier lifestyle.

According to the report, researchers at a Spanish university had found that for every glass of red wine taken a day the risk of contracting lung cancer is lowered by thirteen percent. Beer, spirits and rosé wine offers no such protection, and white wine may well increase the risk. As Pat and Ron are both heavy smokers, they have changed their drinking regime dramatically. Working on the principle that the more red wine they drink the less risk they will run of developing cancer, they intend to get through at least half a dozen bottles of their favourite Cotes du Rhone a day. It will be a demanding schedule, but, as Ron said, nothing is as important as one's health.

As well as Pat and Ron, Dafyd the Welsh statistical wizard, Lonely Eric, Conan the Librarian and the bounteous Veronica, we have a new member for our study group. Dolly is a very nice lady of advanced years who arrived last week to live with her son and daughter-in-law in Sourciéville, and she has already found how the language barrier can lead to confusion and occasional embarrassment.

As she told us with the refreshing candour that age can bring, Dolly registered with her local doctor shortly after her arrival and was asked by the English-speaking receptionist if she would like a general health check. She agreed, and was ushered in to the surgery to meet the young doctor. The receptionist having left to answer a call and the doctor speaking as little English as she did French, the two had to communicate by sign language. Having taken her pulse, examined her eyes, tested her hearing and made some notes while waiting for the return of their interpreter, the doctor indicated that she should go over to a corner of the room. Seeing a screen against the wall and thinking the doctor was going to conduct a more thorough examination, she went behind it, then emerged wearing only her Wellington boots as the receptionist returned. After recovering from the shock and persuading the doctor to come out from beneath his desk, the woman explained that her employer had actually asked Dolly to go and stand by the wall so he could measure her height.

When I sympathised and said how embarrassing the incident must have been, Dolly replied quite cheerfully that it had all worked out for the best. As a result of the unexpected revelation, her new doctor had given her a free prescription for a very comfortable and supportive all-over body stocking.

*   *   *   *   *

My fox is enjoying a midnight feast as I tell her about my evening, and unlike the local customers at the Bar des Amis she clearly has no prejudices against English food. The vixen will need all the calories she can get as winter tightens, and has already enjoyed four of my wife's sausage rolls and an interesting slab of savoury pickle-flavoured bread pudding made by Dolly, who said she had thought the unmarked jar in her daughter-in-law's cupboard contained mincemeat.

While the fox makes a start on a selection of savoury pastries formed and baked into disconcertingly phallic shapes by Veronica, I consider how the evening has crystallised the differences in culture and magnified the entrenched attitudes of the two communities. A Martian dropping in to the Bar des Amis this evening would have instantly understood why our two nations have been either at arm's length or war for the best part of a thousand years. There may have been other excuses made by the French for all those bloody encounters, but I think our misuse of their language could be at least part of the reason.

The expressions on the faces of the locals changed from bemusement to disbelief and finally undisguised horror as they listened to what some of my students were doing to their tongue, and even the impeccably courteous Henri Charrier visibly blanched at the more extreme assaults. Having caused a few grimaces myself during the evening, I find it a thought-provoking fact that we can never know what our treatment of any foreign language sounds like to its owner. We can generally identify the nationality of a foreigner speaking English, but cannot know how we sound when speaking his language. From what I have observed this evening, perhaps this is for the best.

I also find it puzzling how attractive so many British women think English sounds when mangled by a French man, but I have generally noticed that their appreciation is usually linked directly to the physical attributes of the speaker rather than his vocal delivery. When Henri addressed our class in his deep, slightly accented and cultured tones I thought Veronica was going to swoon, but when Albert Poubelle focused his wandering eye on her cleavage and attempted to tell a risque joke in English, the effect was entirely different.

It did not help with the building of better relationships between the two camps that one of our students had clearly come along determined not to be won over by the benefits of learning the language of the country in which he had chosen to live.

Conan the Librarian had equipped himself with a list of hundreds of words that are the same in English and French, and insisted on reading them out before the lesson began. Having droned on for half an hour, he then showed us a passage in a textbook that claimed that understanding five hundred words in any foreign language was enough for the speaker to get by in the country where it is spoken. Ignoring my point that our having words like agglomeration and Monegasque in common with the French would not be much help when passing the time of day with a neighbour or asking for the loan of a monkey-wrench, he retired to the bar and spent the rest of the evening drinking the free wine and complaining about the illogicality of his hosts' language and culture. Like many would-be students of a foreign language, he obviously finds it impossible to simply accept another nation's rules of grammar, syntax and general usage. He seemed determined to undermine the whole purpose of the event, and at one stage I thought there was going to be an outbreak of violence when he used Dafyd as an interpreter to tell Albert Poubelle that his surname is a derogatory word in English.

Overall, I do not think that we have advanced the cause of amity between the locals and incomers; but I think some bridges may have been built. Most of the class have said they will come to next week's lesson, and some have said they will use the bar more often and do their best to speak to the locals in their own language. Veronica seemed the most anxious to improve her language skills and general Anglo-Franco relations during her husband's absence, and after Henri Charrier told her he had to get home in time for an intimate supper with his boyfriend, she accepted a lift on Albert's tractor.

The evening also gave me the opportunity to put my puppy plan into action. After we had been thrashed by the locals in a fairly friendly game of darts and they had pretended to be interested in the English buffet, I asked Madame Poelet to bring Eric's surprise present from the back room. When he saw the baby terrier and realised it was for him, his face became a battleground of emotions. I could see that his head was considering the emotional as well as physical cost of taking on the responsibility, but his heart was the eventual winner. At first he said that he did not want or need another dog and Scotty might be jealous of the newcomer, but I said the real dog would be a companion for his imaginary pet. I also told him that the puppy had already been inoculated, would eat little and had a distinguished pedigree. And that having such an endearing and visible pet would guarantee introduction to other dog lovers, especially single women. After another moment of inner struggle, he sighed heavily, took the puppy in his arms and thanked me in a gruff voice. When I left, Eric was showing his pet off to the synchronised drinking team and promising that he would teach the dog to understand French as well as English commands.

How people choose to lead their lives is none of my affair, nor is it my right or responsibility to try and change them. I do not like the current fashion for believing there is a single and simple answer to any problem, but I think and hope my little gesture will do no harm. Whoever they are and whatever their character, it seems to me that everyone needs someone else apart from themselves to care about.

Having enjoyed a second supper with my new friend, I roll a last cigarette before returning to Le Marais. The marshland shimmers in the moonlight, the creatures of the night are going about their business, my fox is replete and another intriguing day of our life in the Cotentin has passed. It has brought us no nearer to achieving our plans for avoiding financial catastrophe, but for the moment it is enough to sit beneath the big Norman sky and thank my lucky stars for finding this most entrancing of places and people.

La belle cage ne nourrit pas l'oiseau.
(A beautiful cage does not feed the bird.)

French proverb

11

It is, as the locals would say, duck cold.

The winter wraiths have been flexing their muscles and showing what they can do when in a bad mood. Quarrelsome winds roam the marsh as if in search of a fight, and the lack of resistance they meet seems to goad them into greater fury. It is a battle just to walk across the treeless expanse, and even the most ardent hunters have been sheltering in their underground bunkers or gathering in local bars to boast about the number of defenceless birds and animals they would have slaughtered if the weather had been kinder. But in spite of their love of killing, all members of the hunting fraternities in our area have been abashed by the news that the last she-bear in the Pyrenees is dead. Those responsible say they opened fire when she charged their dogs during a boar shoot and claim they were acting in self-defence. Whatever the truth, it means that the twelve remaining males in the region will die without issue and a part of the country's natural history and heritage will die with them.

Life goes on in its pleasantly haphazard manner at Le Marais, and one advantage of the freezing weather is that we have an excuse to make the most calorie-laden meals. I know of no more seductive aroma than an applewood fire with a caldron of beef stew and dumplings bubbling above it. Even some of our French visitors have been impressed with what is happening in the kitchen, and yesterday Mr Querville sent his wife to ask for the recipe for whatever was responsible for the *odeur* drifting across the fence. Being French as well as Basque, he naturally claimed the dish was not for personal consumption but that he wanted it to try out on his dogs. When he heard it was an old Glaswegian dish of beef dripping, onions and potato that my grandmother taught me to make, he said that the Scottish race was actually descended from the Basques who colonised that country well before the Picts, so that was obviously where the dish originated.

We have made a start on the stable block in spite of the hostile weather, and our new builder is making good progress. When I told Albert Poubelle about Mr Balourd's accident he said his cousin was looking for work, so we have given him a week's trial.

Clovis is a very large young man with a pleasant manner and seems to know his way around a sledgehammer. His day rate is considerably lower than Mr Balourd's, and as far as I can tell he has all his appendages intact. He is as amiably slipshod and untidy as his predecessor was fastidious, but seems so far to have no death-wish. We shall not know the level of his more advanced construction skills until he has stripped the building of all the old partitioning and dug up the concrete floor, but I shall be able to help him with the finer aspects of plumbing and electrical work when Donella is not at home.

If all goes well we shall have our letting rooms ready for the Christmas holidays, but will need to practice our professional hospitality skills before the official opening. We often had guests at La Puce, but as they were staying for free they could hardly complain about the facilities and levels of service. Even so, they often did.

From what I have heard from those who offer accommodation to their fellow Britons, a dramatic change comes over people who pay to stay in your home. Having studied the market in our area, it seems to me that every expatriate couple with a spare room (and many who have not) have tried their hand at offering *chambres d'hôte* facilities to British tourists. Nearly all have grim tales to tell about paying guests and their annoying little ways. This afternoon we are visiting a Briton who has built up a very successful B &B business, so I hope to learn some tricks of the trade. But first I must make a duty call at the Bar des Amis and The Good Intent to make arrangements for our next exercise in very localised *entente cordiale*.

*   *   *   *   *

Because of the bad weather I find The Bar des Amis unusually busy. Most of the regulars are well beyond retirement age so need no excuse to avoid working, but firewood is expensive and a warm room for the price of a glass or two of wine in company is a comfortable arrangement.

As the bar is so full, I pause at the doorway to flex my fingers and prepare mentally to observe the strict rules of arrival protocol. If I were entering a local in England, a general nod to the other regulars would satisfy custom and courtesy. In France, I must greet each of the customers in the correct order of precedence and with exactly the right degree of familiarity, warmth or respect. And I must also use exactly the right style of handshake. The level of cordiality and firmness of grip will depend on many factors, including the greetee's age, social

163

status and importance to me and my place in the community. I know that some people wonder why French is accepted as the official language of diplomacy around the world, and why the European Union and so many other international bodies choose to practice Gallic rules of protocol. What they do not appreciate is that the French are better than any other race at obfuscation, which my dictionary defines as the art and practice of concealing the meaning of any communication by making it more confusing and harder to interpret. This talent is of course ideally suited to the needs of diplomacy.

Apart from the demands of convention, handshaking is the basic coinage of social interaction in France, and nowhere more than in rural France. I have even seen ultra-traditionalists shake hands with every other customer in a bar after he has made a brief visit to the toilet. Some foreign cynics claim the custom developed because the French are so naturally rude and thoughtless that the ritual was needed to mask these traits. I think this is a harsh view, and that - as with their attitude to bureaucracy - they just like ritual in their daily lives.

Since becoming a regular at the Bar des Amis, I have graduated some way from the stranger's neutral nod and greeting. Protocol now permits and requires me to shake the hands of all regulars on the premises, excepting the owner. This is partly because she is a woman, but in any case Madame Poelet will have her hands occupied with cooking implements at whatever time I arrive. If there are strangers (e.g. residents of a nearby village) present, the strict rules of engagement do not allow me to shake their hands, and they would be surprised and perhaps even offended if I did so before a proper introduction. A nodded and verbal acknowledgement is, however *de rigeur*. This admission price to a simple country bar may seem unnecessarily taxing and even petty in its application, but I find any human contact preferable to the pretence that those around you do not exist. The last time I visited London I tried greeting every person I met while walking down a quiet street, and was met mostly with suspicious and sometimes angry looks. One woman even threatened to report my unwanted approach to a policeman if she could have found one.

.

I have reached the table where the synchronised drinking and smoking team are in full session, and am about to reach out a hand when the trio lay down their cigarettes, hold their glasses up in my direction and say a word in their usual faultless unison. The word appears to be English, and, allowing for French pronunciation, sounds remarkably like 'bollocks'. When I ask for a replay, I find this is actually what the group said. When I ask why, they look rather hurt and their spokesman says they thought I would be pleased they were making the effort to make me feel at home. Apparently, Conran the Librarian has had a change of heart about my plans for bringing the two communities together, and has started giving lessons in colloquial English to the regulars at The Bar des Amis. Yesterday the subject was informal greetings, and he spent an hour coaching the synchronised drinking team in what he said was a typically friendly salutation in public bars across the United Kingdom.

*   *   *   *   *

Despite all its good intentions, the Entente Cordiale will never fulfil its ambition to bridge the gap between our two communities and cultures; or at least not in the hands of its present owners.

There is a new lock on the door, and above it a notice informing all clientele that there will be no more opening or closing times at The Good Intent. The notice gives no further details, but it seems obvious that Simon has run out of enthusiasm or money for his adventure, or perhaps both. As his wife has also run out on him, I can only imagine how he is feeling now that both his dream and marriage lie in ruins.

Pressing my face against the window, I can see that the fixtures and furnishings are still all in place and it is only the customers who are missing. The farm implements remain displayed artfully on the walls, the stools lined up at the bar and the shelves stocked with bottles and glasses. Even more poignantly, the sign above the servery is still announcing that Every Hour is Happy Hour at the Entente Cordiale. It is sad to think that the owner has decided to call time for the last time and just walked away. Wherever he has gone, I hope Simon will recover from the triple whammy of losing his business, his dream and his wife.

As I turn away, the old dog from next door arrives to see what I am doing. We exchange looks and I attempt a version of an advanced Gallic shrug which will convey regret at the outcome of a well-intended if doomed experiment. The dog does not respond beyond a grunt, but if he were human I would interpret his expression as one of grim satisfaction.

*   *   *   *   *

Leaving Clovis happily demolishing the concrete floor in the stable block, we are on our way to pick up some tips about running a successful bed-and-breakfast business. As we drive past hedgerows which appear to have been dusted with icing sugar, I have been reporting on the closure of the British pub. Donella has told me that Jonathan Kerr wishes to meet me at a bar in Sourciéville this evening. My wife said he would not say what he wanted to talk about, only that it was an idea which could be of advantage to us and our situation. She added that, as he helped Simon ruin himself financially at the Good Intent and stole his wife into the bargain, she would far rather take heed of even my wildest proposals than his. I know that my wife has a low opinion of my friend, but I think she may be misjudging him because of his affair with Saskia. I have frequently observed how women can be quite illogical when it comes to assessing people's character.

Now that work is under way on our own venture, I am looking forward to meeting the owner of the thriving B&B near Sourciéville. After the collapse of the Entente Cordiale, it will be reassuring to meet someone who has proved that a Briton can run a successful business in France.

According to a television news item this morning, the prospects for modest British enterprises in this country are not encouraging. Using the Haute Vienne area as an example, the presenter said that more than a hundred Britons had registered small businesses with the local authorities in the last six months. Wearing the same smug expression as the dog outside the Good Intent, he added that past evidence indicated that ninety percent of these *petites entrerprises* will go bankrupt within the next five years. This statistic took no account of the number of unregistered British businesses which fail, so the percentage of actual disasters is certain to be even higher.

With even more relish, a regional reporter then took up the story in the neighbouring Dordogne, where half the British-run businesses in the region had gone bust in less than a year of setting up. Examples of those expatriates who had seen their dreams turn into nightmares included a retired teacher who opened a gourmet restaurant in a former cow shed, and a one-time computer analyst who wanted to bring the benefits of Tantric yoga to rural France. Trying his best to look concerned for the destitute expatriates, the presenter in the studio concluded that Britain (as the great Napoleon Bonaparte said) is still obviously a nation of small shopkeepers at heart. With lip-smacking relish he concluded that the problems experienced by so many Britons trying to set up shop in France indicated that what they had to sell was just not wanted by the French... or even by their fellow English expatriates.

The ancient Land Rover is apparently trying to climb over a broken fence. The fence surrounds a paddock in which sit a series of obstacles the vehicle has obviously encountered en route to its present situation. Sitting at the wheel is a blindfolded man, while a young woman at his side appears to be telling him what she thinks of his driving ability. By the gate to the paddock, a number of people are watching the scene with that curious mixture of embarrassment and poorly disguised relish which indicates they are British. If French, they would be making no attempt to hide their pleasure at witnessing the small but juicy domestic drama. Near the group, a very large and dishevelled man is shouting at the couple through the sort of tin megaphone seen in old film footage of the University Boat Race. Eventually, the man in the Land Rover rips off his blindfold, jumps to the ground and stalks off towards the big house beyond the paddock. The young woman follows, pausing only to stoop and pick up a clod of earth to throw at him.

While we discuss the various scenarios that could have led to the situation, the man with the megaphone detaches himself from the party and shambles amiably over to ask our business. As he approaches I am put in mind of a large and particularly badly-groomed bear that has just emerged backwards from a very dense bush. He is tall and broad and most of his peculiarly wedge-shaped head is covered with a grizzled grey pelt of cropped hair and beard. What can be seen of his face reveals a dedicated drinker's florid complexion, a disproportionally small, snout-like nose, and a pair of button-bright eyes beneath a contiguous hedge of eyebrow.

Despite the man's appearance, his body language is not aggressive. But below a stained string vest, he is wearing one of the most intimidating pair of shorts I have ever seen. They are roughly the same colour and texture as the clod of earth the woman threw at her companion, and so rigid that they could be made of tin plating. If mediaeval armourers ever made customised leg wear for jousting tournaments in a heatwave, they would have looked exactly like this remarkable garment.

Seeing my apprehensive look, our host adjusts his crotch, belches absent-mindedly and explains that he has worn the shorts every day since his wife left him, which was, to the best of his recollection, around six years ago. He does not make it clear whether his wife left him because of the condition of his shorts, or that their condition has resulted from her departure. The amiable giant goes on to say that his shorts have deliberately not been laundered in that time, and what began as a lack of concern over personal hygiene has become a sort of tradition. He has grown to love them and their condition, and they have become part of him and his persona. He had considered having them refurbished some years ago, but a survey amongst his regular guests showed they liked the unchanging nature of his appearance together with what he has to offer at the *Maison des Fous.*

Having learned who we are, apologised for forgetting our appointment and introduced himself, our ursine host invites us to join him for a drink in the house. Keeping upwind, we follow him and his creaking shorts through the magnificent arched portico of what looks like a former presbytery which has been savaged by a clutch of crazed interior decorators after overdosing on one too many television makeover programmes. As we pass a classic eighteenth-century bureau which has been painted a virulent pink, Roly Rufus explains that we have just missed the final of this week's Obstacle Race.

The rules, he says, are quite simple, and participation mandatory. The aim of the competition is for the blindfolded male driver to successfully navigate the course as his partner gives directions on how to avoid the obstacles. In practice, the event inevitably ends in a huge row between the most amicable of couples. As normal, the man blames the woman for her navigating, while she blames him for either not following or

169

even *for* following her instructions. The event, our host says while filling two bucket-sized wine glasses, helps to break the ice and allows the house guests to get to know each other. When I ask him if there is not a risk of the altercations spoiling his guests' holiday, he shrugs his massive shoulders and says that is part of the fun. Scratching his beard, he says anecdotal evidence suggests that the blindfold driving contest has been responsible for at least three separations and two divorces, but he believes that to be an exaggeration.

We settle down on a leather sofa which looks as if it has been patched with a previous pair of our host's shorts, and he tells his story.

Once upon a time he was a lecturer in mechanical engineering at a technical college in Swindon. His wife was a schoolteacher at a local primary school. Before they were driven mad by their jobs, they decided to move to France and set up a *gite* and bed and breakfast enterprise. They had visited dozens of English-run establishments over the years and could not see how they could make any worse a job of it than the owners of some of the places at which they had stayed. Unfortunately, they did. While he enjoyed the life and meeting new people, the pressures of keeping him and the house clean and fielding the complaints from the guests was too much for his wife. Also, as more and more Britons set up shop in the area and fought over the available trade, bookings fell off and the money ebbed away. Eventually, his wife left him and went back to teaching in England.

Alone in the big house, he lost interest in even pretending to care about giving the occasional visitors what they thought they wanted. Rather than putting on a show, he would just be himself. Astonishingly, the more outrageous his behaviour, the more his guests returned. They also told their friends about the big mad man in the big mad house, and further paying customers arrived to see if the standards of catering, hospitality and hygiene could possibly be as bad as described. Now he is fully booked the year round, and some people return in spite of (or even because of) their experiences.

Roly does not know if his style of management would work for other establishments, but what he calls the Fawlty Towers approach has worked for him. People, he concludes after pouring me another bucket's-worth of wine, are funny. If you try too hard, they look for something to complain about. If you obviously don't give a toss and act as if they are lucky to be allowed to buy what you are selling, they queue up for it. Life, says our host with his button eyes shining somehow sadly, can be strange like that.

I think of the fate of Simon and his efforts to bridge the culture gap with the Entente Cordiale and lift my glass in admiration. I also see my wife looking from our host to me, and think I know what she is thinking. Whatever happens with our plans for Le Marais, I don't think Donella will be persuaded that I should emulate our host and try to attract hordes of customers just by being myself.

*   *   *   *   *

It is mid-afternoon and, apart from the owner and I, the bar in Sourciéville is empty. Somehow it feels more than empty. It is one of the few bars in the area I have not visited before, and is obviously a local's local. In rural Normandy, this often means that the proprietor has either another source of income with which to subsidise the running of the bar, or is an elderly lady who owns the freehold of the building and enjoys passing her remaining days being rude to a handful of male regulars. Most of these formidable ladies are widows, so perhaps it is a convenient arrangement to allow them to practise the skills of attrition developed over a long marriage. Curiously, the male customers who patronise these sorts of bars seem to enjoy being at the sharp end of the owner's tongue, so perhaps they view their local as a true home-from-home.

Having no other customers to berate, Madame has been warming up on me, and I have already been goaded into asking if she is by any chance a descendant of the Parisienne speed-knitting champion, Madame Lafarge. Apparently, the proprietor has either not read *A Tale of Two Cities* or does not understand my clumsy French, so a prickly truce prevails.

I am here to meet Jonathan Kerr, while Donella has returned to Le Marais to check on Clovis's progress. She has left me with a ten euro note and explicit instructions not to agree to any proposals I may receive from my friend the, as she put it, so-called property developer and business consultant. As a parting shot, she reminded me that if I am really intent on finally ruining our financial situation, the best person to ask for advice would be myself.

As I nurse my beer and try to think up some effective repartee in case of another strafing attack from Madame, the door opens to admit what I at first think is a large and colourful bush. I then realise it is a moustache which is impressive even by rural Norman standards. Attached to it is a small man wearing a paint-encrusted pair of overalls which look almost as eyewateringly rigid as the shorts of the owner of the *maison de fous*.

When the man reaches the bar I see he has apparently been using his moustache as a paint brush, and that the top of his shaven head is tinted an interesting shade of gentian. From each ear hangs a large curtain ring, and he is sporting a very impressive black eye.

Ignoring my greeting, the man throws a handful of crumpled banknotes on to the counter. Madame puts them in a jar by the cupboard drawer which she uses as a cash register, then climbs on to a chair and unhooks a large painting from the wall behind the bar. I have been idly regarding the work as I wait for Jonathan, and have concluded that it represents either a very loose impression of sunset over the marshlands, or a fried egg about to slip off a cracked green plate.

Silently, Madame passes the painting across the bar, and

the man holds it at arm's length and regards it with an expression which combines pride, affection and wistfulness. After a moment he returns the canvas and watches as the proprietor re-hangs it. I think about pointing out that she has replaced it upside down - or at any rate in the opposite vertical plane to which it was hanging previously - but as the man makes no comment I hold my peace. After climbing down, Madame pours two large glasses of *pastis* and places them on the counter in front of her customer. She then takes a note from the jar and puts it in the money drawer. The man swallows one drink, steps carefully one pace to his right and drinks the other, wipes his moustache, turns and walks out of the door.

The little tableau has the air of a much-practised routine, so I go to the bar and offer Madame a drink before asking her to explain. The large brandy she serves herself finishes off my ten euro fund, but seems to mellow her mood. Having recharged her glass and pointedly avoided my empty one, she says she is surprised I have not heard of Xavier, who is the town's artist-in-residence. For most of the month, she adds with a disapproving shrug, his precise residence is in the drunk tank in the local *gendarmerie.*

Like so many artists, Xavier has too much of a liking for strong drink. This flaw deters him from his work, and to her knowledge he has only produced the one painting. In a moment of weakness when he was penniless and desperate for a drink, she bought his life's work for the equivalent of twenty euros. He spent the money in one session in her bar, then returned to buy the painting back when his social security cheque arrived. Finding himself without funds a day later, he reappeared with the painting and re-sold it to her. This arrangement carried on for several years, until they both decided there was little point in him ferrying the painting back and forward. Now his sole contribution to the pictorial arts hangs more or less permanently on the wall, and is redeemed for a few moments every time Xavier is in funds. It is, Madame concludes, a very satisfactory arrangement. She has a painting to cover a hole in the wall that her late husband was too lazy to repair, and the lease-lend arrangement ensures that Xavier does all his social drinking in her bar.

When I ask Madame if she likes the painting, she looks at me as if I have made an indecent proposal. Being a student of history and men, she has observed that most of France's great artists were untalented and eccentric alcoholic males who died relatively young. More importantly, their work was invariably ridiculed while they were alive yet became priceless after their death. From what she has seen of the works of the likes of Gauguin and the foreigner Van Gogh, they are no better and certainly no worse than the painting on her wall. She has cornered the market by owning the only canvas that Xavier is likely to produce, and given his rate of consumption it is quite likely she will outlive him. Besides, it is good to feel that she is helping a struggling artist, is a patron of the arts and may even go down in history as the sponsor of a great talent.

When I enquire about her protégé's black eye, coloured head and preference for twin glasses of *pastis*, I realise that the apparent fashion for imaginary companions is not restricted to the expatriate community in this area.

Xavier, Madame explains as she looks meaningfully at her empty glass, has no friends, so invented one several years ago. Understandably, the couple are constant companions and share the same penchant for strong drink. Normally they get on well, but fell out last week over a game of pool. When accused of cheating by going out of turn, Xavier punched his opponent in the face, which of course also belonged to him. His phantom friend responded by running amok in the artist's studio and tipping a pot of paint over Xavier's head, and when order was restored both agreed that the hue suited his image.

*   *   *   *   *

We are on our way home, and I am feeling guilty.

It is a long time since I deliberately deceived my wife on an important matter, though this is mainly because she is far too clever to allow me to keep secrets from her. I am also feeling frustrated because I want to tell Donella about my meeting with Jonathan and his exciting business proposition, but already know what her reaction would be. What I am bursting to tell her is that I have been invited to become the new landlord of the Entente Cordiale.

I have already run a pub in England, but even the experience of trying to keep order in a corner local in a rough area of a naval city has not cured me of my fascination with the licensed profession. Unlike Simon and so many Britons who dream of running a hotel or restaurant or pub in France, I actually know what a life behind bars can be like. It is my belief that everyone who enjoys visiting public houses believes that they could do a much better job of running one than the proprietor of their local. Or any other pub, come to that. In my experience, they are invariably wrong. During our years behind bars I learned to our cost that all the money crossing the counter does not go into the pocket of the proprietor, and that being mine host in a pub is not remotely like entertaining friends at home.

But, even though I made such a hash of it in England, the idea of being a licensee still attracts me; especially the idea of being a licensee on this side of the Channel. Also, and as Jonathan says, with my knowledge of this area of France and the sort of people who live here, I will be able to avoid the mistakes that Simon made.

Best of all and unlike all my past attempts to give Donella security, I will not be risking any of the money we do not have. Jonathan's idea is that we should invite a number of the customers of the Entente Cordiale to form a *pot commune*.

This is a not uncommon arrangement in rural France which involves villagers getting together to save their local bar when the owner has had enough of trying to make ends meet.

The usual system is for an owning committee to be set up, with members buying shares. This provides the pot of money with which to buy the premises and stock. If the business will not bear the cost of professional staffing, the members of the commune will take turns in manning the bar. Apart from providing a facility which would otherwise have been lost, the scheme also has the attraction of giving the members a good excuse to visit the bar more often than their spouses would normally permit. Being the owners, it also means that the committee can bar anyone they do not want frequenting the premises. This inevitably leads to intrigue, internecine feuding and all sorts of other skulduggery, which in many small village communities would naturally be seen as another advantage of the scheme. Best of all from our point of view, the project will not cost me a penny, and I will actually be paid for helping the investors run the Good Intent properly and thus successfully. This time, I just cannot lose.

But I feel that now is not the time to mention Jonathan's proposal. When asked about my meeting, I told Donella that he wanted to see me to talk about his affair with Saskia. I will wait until exactly the right moment to tell her about our plan to re-open the British Bar.

Dusk is falling as we arrive at the gates to Le Marais, and I am pleased to see Clovis's old van parked in the yard. If he is making good progress and Donella is pleased with what he has achieved today, it may be a good time to tell her about Jonathan's proposal.

Pulling up outside the stable block, I see there is a satisfyingly large mound of fragmented concrete, earth and rotten flooring in the yard, and that Clovis is standing beside the pile and holding something muddy in his cupped hands. Even from this distance, I can see that he is handling the object gingerly, and hope it is not an unexploded hand grenade left over from the D-Day Landings.

Raising a hand in greeting, I get out of the car, walk towards him and ask if he has found some hidden treasure. He does not speak, but holds the object towards me. I take it, dig some of the wet earth from a hole in the surface, and find myself in eye-to-socket contact with a human skull.

November is a nice month. But one must like grey.

Gilles Vigneault

12

All is grey.

The notorious Contentin wind is away on business elsewhere, and to stand on our balcony is to be on the bridge of a ship at anchor in a fog-bound sea. Apart from the sharpest yelps from across the fence, barely a sound penetrates the clammy shroud.

Beyond our garden, the *marais* is now a great expanse of water. The constant deluge has soaked the earth and the inland sea has appeared. It is a time of inactivity for those who work the marshes, and also for us and our plans for making a living from our new home.

I am marinating in a bath and thinking of how we can escape financial meltdown while our future B&B business is under strict quarantine regulations. Bright yellow tapes surround the stable block, and inside a trio of white-overalled forensic scientists are using tablespoons where Clovis used a spade. They have located a number of bones which may or may not be related to the skull, and seem disappointed to report that there seem to be no more human remains beneath the soil.

Predictably, the grisly find has been the cause of huge excitement at this normally arid time of year for news. The story of *le crane mystérieux* was splashed on the front page of *Ouest France,* and became the lead item on the regional television news for three days. It is the first time that the village has been mentioned by the media since the curé was defrocked a decade ago, and the local people have milked the situation dry. Our postman tried to sell the inside story of The House of Death to a scandal-rag in Paris, and our neighbour has been accosting and giving interviews to anyone who looks remotely like a reporter. Being a shrewd businessman, Mr Querville ensured he was standing by the notice board on the gate to his kennels when in front of the television cameras, and even credited his giant dog with digging up the skull until Clovis threatened to sue. The local police have also been making the most of their biggest potential crime since a spate of cattle-rustling in the Eighties. Within an hour of my phoning to tell them about the discovery, the stable block, house and lane had been sealed off as if we had found an unexploded bomb rather than a skull. Everyone who lives in the area has been questioned at least twice, and there is a stop-and-search policy operating in the dead-end lane outside Le Marais. So far, nothing more exciting than a dead cat on the back of Albert Poubelle's rubbish cart has been unearthed, but even that discovery found its way into the local newspaper.

Now, all we can do is wait until the investigators have finished their work and made their report. They have been digging up what is left of the earth floor in the stable block, and every ounce will be sifted and examined before being taken away in labelled sacks. As Mr Querville pointed out yesterday in what I think he thought was an attempt to get me to see the bright side of the situation, we are getting this part of our building work done for nothing. Another bonus, he said, is that the fee for the amount of publicity the affair has generated for our bed and breakfast venture would have been in the tens of thousands of euros.

Although no further remains have been found in the stable block, this has not stopped the wildest speculations taking place. Some villagers have been recalling old practices of witchcraft and even human sacrifice, and a particularly well-informed local man is putting it about that the skull may be that of the missing British aristocrat, Lord Lucan.

It will be another month at least before the investigators have finished their work and the remains have been examined in Paris, so it is now certain that our letting rooms will not be ready for the Christmas holidays. This means that Jonathan's proposal has become even more significant, and the launch of the *pot commune* takes place at the Bar Fidele this afternoon.

If the presentation is successful and we take on the Entente Cordiale, one of my first suggestions will be a change of name for the premises. It is said to be unlucky to re-christen boats, but re-naming a failed pub to distance it from its past trading record is standard practice. Given our current situation with the embargoed barn and our dwindling bank balance, I may suggest we call our new venture The Last Chance Saloon.

To take my mind off our financial worries, I have been catching up with my correspondence in my writing shed. Although the sales of my books about trying to make a living in France have not benefited from the huge increase in Britons buying a house in or moving to France, I am now receiving hundreds of e-mails and letters asking for advice or comment. As my wife says, had all those people bought our books and read them, we would be much better off and they would not need to ask me for free advice on how to make a go of living in a foreign land or persuade a local builder to finish their roof. For whatever reason they write, I am flattered that so many people think I should be able to help them, and I always try to respond in a positive way.

A further advantage of this correspondence is the insights I gain on why so many Britons have decided to make - or at least think about making - the move across the Channel.

Settling down in front of the screen, I press the necessary buttons and see that a new correspondent should be placed close to the top of my Unusual Reasons for Choosing an Area of France in Which to Live list. The writer is from the north-east of England, and has chosen to relocate to a village in the Charente. This is not because he particularly likes the weather or topography there when compared with the rest of the country, but because the village bar is owned by a fellow Geordie who stocks Newcastle Brown Ale.

I wish him well and move on to see that an elderly friend from the Aude region has resumed communications. He is a delightfully eccentric character, and begins by apologising for not contacting me for some weeks. He has, he says, had a heavy cold and having heard that viruses can be transmitted by e-mail, did not want me to catch it. He has a very sharp sense of humour, but I am not sure that he is making a joke about giving me his cold.

Another message is from a lady who has bought what she hopes will become an adventure activity centre in the French Alps. All has not gone well with her project, and most of the activity and adventure taking place on the premises for the past month has been altercations with the previous owner of the property. The elderly widow is now claiming that she only sold half of the land and buildings in the deal, and as the local mayor and notaire are her brothers, my correspondent is not hopeful of an amicable settlement. Her only consolation is that the widow has a surname which is quite common in the area, and it is quite satisfying to phone her adversary's home and ask to speak to Mrs Bastard.

*   *   *   *   *

We are at the Bar Fidele in Sourciéville to discuss the forming of the *pot commune*. Madame is so pleased with the unaccustomed custom that she almost smiled at me when I arrived. A special table has been set up in the corner of the bar, and the potential investors in the scheme have arrived. At Jon's suggestion I approached all former customers of the Good Intent, and despite my knowledge of their circumstances and backgrounds I was surprised at some of those who wish to consider becoming our partners.

Although Ron and Pat the former publicans say they are not interested in returning to a life behind bars, they have come along to see what Jonathan has to say while they keep up their health-giving levels of red wine. Lonely Eric, Voluptuous Veronica and Dafyd have also turned up to hear more about the scheme. Making up the party is Conan the Librarian and the nice couple with the imaginary holiday home in our village. Conan says he has always liked the idea of running his own pub, and I suspect his interest stems from him drinking so much that he thinks he might as well have at least a share of the profits on his spending. Phil and Phyllis are sporting matching cardigans, and say that although they are very happy with their virtual property in France, it would be nice to own a part of something more substantial.

As I am about to open the meeting, Veronica leans across the table and tells me she quite fancies the prospect of being a barmaid. I can see that this will suit her personality, and I think her most obvious physical characteristics will certainly be an attraction to male customers at the pub.

Despite his dislike of parting with money, Eric the Lonely says he has come along to consider taking part in the scheme, though I believe he is mainly here for the company and to show off how well he has trained his puppy. When I ask him about Scotty, a shadow crosses his face and he says that his virtual dog became jealous of the new pet and took to disappearing for increasingly long periods. Eventually, he had to choose between the two, and regretfully sold Scotty to a local man. I am not surprised to hear that Eric's customer was Hugo the Not Very Wise. The last time I met Hugo I observed he was wearing odd shoes, and he thought for a full moment before replying that he had another pair just like them at home. I laughed at the old gag, then looked into his eyes and realised he was not joking.

When we are settled, Jonathan introduces himself and his companion. Mr Belette is the estate agent dealing with the sale of the pub, and has come along to answer any questions we may have about the value of the property. As he nods and smiles professionally at the gathering, I see that the elderly *immobilier* sports a set of false teeth which are either one size too big or several sizes too small. Whatever the true discrepancy, they give him the look of a man struggling to finish a piece of sticky toffee pudding before making an after-dinner speech. His close-set eyes also create a furtive air, but this could be the result of becoming an estate agent or the reason he became one.

With the drinks served, Jonathan stands and outlines the proposal in a crisply businesslike manner. As he has already told us, the freehold of The Good Intent is on sale through the offices of Mr Belette, and the price includes all fixtures and fittings and stock. The price also includes the goodwill, he adds with a wry smile, but that will clearly not be worth a great deal.

Regardless of whether any of those present wish to invest, he has already put in an offer for the pub and all its contents, and it has been provisionally accepted by Simon and Saskia. The sale is conveniently being handled by a notaire with whom Jonathan does regular business, and the reasons he intends buying the pub are several.

Firstly, he feels some responsibility towards the previous owners, and secondly he believes that the business has great potential if run and marketed properly. Although there is a traditional French bar in the area, there is certainly room for another licensed business aimed directly at the expatriate community. There has been a considerable influx of British settlers in recent years, and he calculates there are now more than a thousand Britons living within the catchment area of The Good Intent.

The original concept of the Entente Cordiale was honourable, but Jonathan feels that Simon tried too hard to appeal to both communities. That is why he failed. It is his belief that the focus of the new business should be on unashamedly re-creating the atmosphere of the Great British Pub, and that the new Good Intent should be presented as a home-from-home for all British expatriates and visitors. To say that there should not be a British Pub in rural France would be like saying there should be no French-style bars in England, or even any Indian restaurants. While most Britons who settle in France love Camembert and Brie cheese, they still enjoy a slice of Cheddar from time to time.

The third and main reason he is buying the pub has nothing to do with his belief in its commercial promise. With property prices rising so steeply in this part of France, it is a bargain buy and could be sold on at a profit as a potential dwelling house. At this, Jonathan looks to Mr Belette for confirmation, and the estate agent nods so enthusiastically I fear his false teeth will fall out.

So, our host asks rhetorically, if the price and prospects for the Entente Cordiale are so good, why is he inviting us to have a share in the business? To be honest, he has not got a clue about pub operating, and is anyway far too busy with his other interests to involve himself too deeply with the day-to-day running of the premises. Also, if he has learned one thing in his business dealings, it is that people with a stake in any venture always put the most effort and imagination into the project. Besides, the idea of a *pot commune* appeals to him as much as he thinks it will appeal to us potential shareholders. The part-owners of the pub and business will have a direct interest in the success of the venture, and a minimum risk on their investment. The enterprise will be both an enjoyable hobby and a potentially very rewarding project.

As to the level of investment and other arrangements, our chairman proposes a limit of ten shares, each valued at the euro equivalent of twenty thousand pounds. This would cover the agreed price of the freehold and all its fixtures and furnishing, together with legal costs and commissions to the agent. As the proposer of the pot commune and to show his faith in the future of the new bar, Jonathan will take up four of the shares, and the remaining six will be offered to those attending the meeting this evening. If all or any of us decide against joining the scheme, the shares will be offered to other resident Britons, but only those approved of by existing members. As Jonathan points out, the division and number of shares allocated will mean that, although the major stakeholder in the company, he could always be outvoted on matters of policy by a bloc formed by other members. If for any reason a shareholder should want to leave the syndicate, he or she would be repaid their original investment, plus any profits accruing from trading or increase in property prices. So once again, the risk factor for investors will be minimised.

The finer details of how the *pot commune* would be set up and run will be agreed at a later date, and each of us has a week to decide whether to come on board. Jonathan has a list of other Britons who have expressed interest in the scheme, and will shortly be sounding them out. It is, of course, important that we move quite swiftly, lest a better offer be made for the freehold of the Entente Cordial. The offer he has put in is, as he said earlier, a very good one from a buyer's point of view, and it would be a pity if another party were to hear about the availability of the property and business and make a move. At this point, Jonathan looks meaningfully at us and then at Mr Belette. While not actually laying a finger alongside his nose and winking conspiratorially, the estate agent gives a double click of his dentures and manages to convey the impression that he will not be making much of an effort to find another buyer for the Entente Cordial.

On a practical note, our host adds, we must also move quickly if we want the bar to be re-opened in time for Christmas. We will all know how long it can take to make things happen when officialdom is involved, and even more so with the public holidays looming. As well as the actual property purchase, there will be the complicated business of applying for a transfer of licence; this is another reason he is employing the services of a friendly and influential out-of-town notaire.

Finally, he would like to make two further important proposals to the potential board. As he said earlier, he does not know anything about running pubs, but we all know a man who does. Regardless of our enthusiasm for the project, we will need professional guidance to make a real success of the former Entente Cordial. Therefore, he intends offering me the position of manager of the new pub. Furthermore, he proposes that a perfect name for our British pub would be the George Inn.

*   *   *   *   *

I am sharing the good news with my vulpine friend. We are also sharing a cold bacon sandwich as I tell her that I and the rest of the members of the pot commune have been sworn to secrecy, but I don't think our chairman will object to me explaining the project to a fox. I will lay out Jonathan's proposals in detail tomorrow to Donella, and this rehearsal by the river will be good practice. I will take my wife to lunch so that we will be in relaxed surroundings, and the location will also mean she will not be able to shout at me if my presentation is not well received. Having said that, I do not see how even my wife can disapprove of my being paid for spending time on licensed premises.

Even better news about the project is that as well as having the first (as he called it) anglo-pub in Normandy named after me, I will be allowed to buy one of Jonathan's shares from my wages. As our chairman says, I will have even more incentive for making The George a raging success if I have a stake in the business, and the potential for our scheme is not limited to a single outlet. When the pub has got off the ground, he will expect me to travel around Normandy locating and setting up new English-style pubs. As well as finding the sites and investors, I will also be liaising with the media and could become quite a celebrity. As he says, I have shown in the past that my strengths are in publicity, marketing and hands-on operations rather than the unimaginative realms of hard business, so we should make an ideal partnership of talents.

Perhaps surprisingly, it seems that we shall have no lack of investors for the proposed chain. All those at the presentation expressed strong interest, Conan asked if he could buy two shares, and even Eric said he would like to become a stakeholder - though he only wishes to buy a tenth of a share.

After we had toasted the future of The George with probably the first bottle of champagne the owner of the Bar Fidele has served to paying customers, we made an appointment for our next meeting before the other members of the pot commune left with Mr Belette.

When he had told me about my shareholding and his plans for the chain of anglo-pubs, Jonathan said how pleased he was that our paths had crossed. Quite apart from my being exactly the right person to make his vision a reality, he was particularly happy that he would be able to help my wife and me through a bad time in our lives. Like me, Jonathan is still undecided whether our futures are guided by fate or self-determination, but whatever the spur, he feels that our meeting will bring about a great change in both our lives.

I toss another strip of bacon across the river and the fox catches it with practiced ease. Although I think we have grown close in the past months and she accepts me and appears almost immediately I whistle, she is still a wild animal and I think it important she remains one. I have deliberately not given her a name and must not get too close to her. It will be sad if she does not appear at our rendezvous one evening, but the odds are that it will happen, and I must accept that this is the way of nature.

An antidote to our disastrous dinner at Sourciéville earlier this year... and another very good reason for living in rural France.

To broach the news about the pot commune and my involvement to my wife, I announced over breakfast that I was taking her to lunch. Many women would be disappointed to learn they were being dined at the French equivalent of a transport café, but Donella was delighted. She knows that not only will the meal be almost ridiculously cheap, but that the lunchtime special in the renowned if unofficial *relais routier* we shall be visiting puts even the swankiest restaurants in the region to shame. And as I have heard so many Normans observe, a meal tastes so much better when the bill is no more than the cost of making it at home.

*   *   *   *   *

Our luncheon venue is unprepossessing in appearance, and to the uninformed passer-by would look more like an abandoned grocery shop than a centre of culinary excellence.

On a minor road made virtually redundant by the autoroute channelling commercial traffic to and from Cherbourg, the dilapidated building bears no advertising blurbs, or even a name. Except for a grubby set of net-curtaining, the windows are bare, and there are no clues to what delights lie beyond the rickety front door. It is almost as if the owners want to keep all evidence of their success to themselves. For certain, they prefer to keep the good news from the tax authorities, and all bills at this establishment are settled on a strictly cash-only basis. Though short on visual appeal and marketing materials, the restaurant has probably the biggest and fullest car park in the area, and this is as ever the best advertisement for what it is selling. What is on offer at The Stuffed Goose (as it is known to those in the know) is probably the worst-kept secret in all Lower Normandy as far as lovers of good and plentiful food are concerned.

Pulling into one of the few remaining spaces, I see that not much work will be going on in homes, offices and shops across the region for at least the next two hours.

The car park is an eclectic jumble of tradesmen's vans, delivery vehicles, smart and dilapidated cars, and there is even a donkey cart moored to the broken fence skirting a stream alongside the café. As my wife rummages in her mobile feeding station for a carrot, I pass the time of day with the animal and am rewarded with no more than a mournful stare. Although he might not appreciate the finer points of what is happening inside the café, he will know that he is in for a long wait. The donkey will also need no assistance in finding the route home, which is probably why the owner has chosen this mode of transport.

Opening the door like a chef lifting the lid on a pot containing his *pièce de résistance* for the day, I savour the complementary bouquets of classic country cooking, strong tobacco and craftsmen's lived-in overalls. Standing to one side, I bow my wife in, loosen my belt and wave to the donkey as we enter.

*   *   *   *   *

Inside, at least fifty customers jostle amiably for elbow space at the rows of tables laid out in banqueting-style formation. But this is not the usual composition of diners one would expect to meet in a British restaurant. Plumbers break bread with bank managers, postmen rub shoulders with mayors, and I know from the vehicles outside that there are at least two septic tank cleaning specialists amongst this happy throng. In England they would not be allowed to set foot on the premises. Here they wear their overalls and piquant odour with pride, and are welcomed by the management and even those who sit next to them on the severe benches.

This seating and social arrangement is another sure sign of a really good *routier*, as the diners obviously value the quality of food above class divisions and the privacy of separate tables. A further telling indication of the standards of the catering is the sheer size as well as number of the diners. There is hardly a man in the room who is under fifteen stone, and for once I feel almost slender. Most of the pairs of buttocks spreading unconcernedly across the narrow tops of the benches would require two sturdy bar stools to play a proper supporting role.

In spite of being at such close quarters to their fellow diners, the customers at The Stuffed Goose are also demonstrating the Gallic defence of *laissez-faire* and the freedom of the individual to go to the devil in his own way, and the air is thick with cigarette smoke. In some areas the visibility is down to less than a yard, and some patrons must be eating by radar. Although smoking in restaurants has been technically banned for more than a decade, here it appears a compulsory accompaniment to the food.

Amongst the sea of masculinity, a single young woman moves effortlessly about her business. I sometimes wonder where women eat at lunchtime in our part of France, but it is rarely in this sort of establishment. But this girl is not demeaned by her solitary serving role. In fact, she is demonstrating the arts and crafts of her profession with pride. Like an ice skater showing her paces, she glides down the aisles, gracefully bending at the waist to gather an empty plate and lay down a full one - and with never a single mistake. At the same time she is replenishing glasses and taking fresh orders, delivering bills, accepting payments and even finding time to play her part in at least twenty ongoing conversations. She will pick up where she left off at each one without a trace of uncertainty or hesitation. Amongst a host of craftsmen and professionals she is more than an equal, and exults in this daily opportunity to prove it.

Sensing my admiring gaze, the waitress makes change from the pouch at her waist, tops up a trio of glasses, chides a huge man in a bib and brace overall for not clearing his plate, then leads us to a space near the bar. A menu materialises in my hand, a dirty ashtray is whisked away and replaced, a jug of iced water and two glasses appear in front of us, and we are left to get to know the *carte* and our neighbours.

As I squeeze my way on to the bench, I see that one of those neighbours is the superintendent at our local rubbish tip, and that he is having a working lunch. Across the table from Mr Tyran is his *aide-de-campe*, a man with more pens in the breast pocket of his jacket than teeth in his head. Both are wearing their official commune hats at a rigidly formal angle, so serious business as well as pleasure must be on the agenda. On the table between them is a sheet of paper bearing a list of names, some of which I recognise as members of our commune. Several of the names are marked with ticks or crosses, while four have a red line drawn through them. Trying not to look as if I am looking, I scan the list over the top of my menu and am irrationally relieved to see that my name warrants neither a cross, star or line. It is possible that the supremo of the *décheterie* and his camp commandant are merely updating their directory of permit holders, and that the crossed-out names belong to members of the commune who have moved or passed away. Knowing how Yves Tyran views the responsibilities of his customers, however, it is quite possible that the list is some sort of behavioural assessment. The owners of those names bearing ticks could have distinguished themselves by their conduct while at the tip, while those with crosses will have somehow broken one of many rules of engagement as laid down by the superintendent and backed with the full force of the Fourth Republic. Those unfortunates who have had their names crossed out may even have been excommunicated for some transgression, and will shortly be left to wander forever in the wastelands of the Cotentin in search of somewhere to dump their redundant household effects.

Looking up and catching Mr Tyran's eye, I smile ingratiatingly and nod to the wine pitcher alongside the list. It is, I say, almost empty, and I would be honoured if he would permit me to fill it. He gives me a hard look, then shakes his head. As I turn to signal to the waitress that we are ready to order, I see that he has given some sort of silent instruction to his assistant. Mr Brunnez whips a pen from its billet with practised ease, looks at his boss for confirmation, then makes a mark on the list. I cannot see if he is using the deadly red pen, or what mark he is making where. With luck he is adding a tick to my name; at worst my open attempt at bribery and possible corruption has added me to the list of the damned.

As our waitress glides our way, I feel other eyes on me and see Jonathan Kerr watching from a nearby table. At first he appears ill-at-ease, then smiles and waves. He is in company with Mr Belette and another equally weaselly-featured man. Perhaps the two are related, or more likely the stranger is another estate agent whose face proclaims his calling.

Jonathan half-rises and waves as if he would like us to join him. I snatch a look at my wife and shake my head in warning. I have every intention of telling Donella about the pot commune today, but not until the food and drink has put her in the most receptive of moods.

*   *   *   *   *

An hour later and I am suffering from a surfeit of curiosity and pure greed. I have also learned why so many of the customers make me look almost anorexic.

Having discarded the menu and given ourselves into the

hands of our waitress, we started with thick tranches of a terrine which was as unappetising in its grey colour as it was exquisite in taste. The French do not always eat with their eyes, despite what you usually see on a plate in a fancy restaurant. When I asked the waitress for its provenance, she was apparently so surprised and delighted to find a Briton interested in what he had been eating that she summoned the cook and owner. They were the same person, and embodied in the sturdy frame of a middle-aged lady with the face of a Madonna and arms of a docker. Rather than the recipe, the lady was carrying a huge pot of the terrine so that we could further acquaint ourselves with the taste as she talked us through the details of ingredients and construction. To refuse another helping would have seemed churlish, and then she insisted I try another slice to fully appreciate her comments on consistency and content.

Clearly, I should have said nothing when we had encountered the main course of black pudding, apple and onion in a Calvados sauce, but good manners required me to send my compliments to the kitchen. Once again, Madame emerged with seconds... and then thirds. The more I cleared my plate, the more she filled it. And so the game went on.

Either the lady saw me as an inquisitive English gastronaut, a hopeless gourmand, or just a challenge. Whatever the reason, I felt obliged to eat for England. As time passed and the bench groaned piteously beneath me, other diners began to take an interest in the contest. Without becoming distracted from their own plates, our nearest neighbours would offer encouragement and advice; others further afield would send messages of congratulation with the waitress.

Eventually, I borrowed a white handkerchief from my wife and waved it in submission. As a round of spontaneous applause broke out, I dragged myself to the counter to thank our hosts. I had eaten enough for five, and paid the price of a mediocre starter in a mid-range restaurant in Paris.

Before leaving, I asked Madame where she had learned to cook, and if Normandy was her home territory. I should not have been surprised to learn that the owner of *L'oie Bourrée* had picked up her skills and inclinations from her home town of Riberac. That part of France is renowned for the quality of its *foie gras*, and that quality is achieved by force-feeding geese to achieve the largest and tenderest livers in all France.

I am unsure about my liver, but my belly is now occupying at least twice the space it did before entering the restaurant. As I concentrate on navigating my way through the remaining vehicles without causing damage to their or my bodywork, I reflect that I at least had the option to refuse Madame's instinctive desire to see her charges stuffed to beyond repletion.

Etendez vos pieds selon la couverture.
(Stretch out your feet according to the blanket.)

Norman proverb

13

The year nears its end, and the countryside is in sombre mood. The sky above Le Marais is the colour of flint, and I think a storm may be brewing.

I have yet to tell Donella about the pot commune, but will do so after my meeting with Jonathan Kerr this morning. There is still no news of when we can re-start work on the stable block, and I feel a general sense of foreboding about our future. It might be the weather or our bank balance which is causing my melancholia, and I am sure I will snap out of it when we launch The George.

Looking at our latest bank statement, I think about following Barbara West's example and consigning it to the fire. But even out of sight it would not be out of mind. Sometimes when I am in this black mood I think how much easier our lives might have been if we had stayed in England. We could certainly have been no worse off financially, and may even have prospered. But then, as my wife reminds me when the black dog is at my shoulder, we only paint bright pictures of what might have been. And had we stayed in England, we would never have known The Little Jewel and La Puce or met René

Ribet and all our friends in Lower Normandy. I am reminded of an entrepreneurial friend who was fond of saying that people who don't take risks don't make mistakes, but neither do they make money or have any fun. I agreed with him then, though the last time we met was to drown his sorrows after he had declared himself bankrupt for the fifth time and his third wife had declared herself fed up with him and run away with her personal fitness and lifestyle consultant.

On balance I would not have missed our fifteen years of small adventuring in France; but it would have been nice to have been more than just one step ahead of financial ruin along the way.

*   *   *   *   *

Arriving at Sourciéville, my mood brightens as the latest highway *spectacle* is in the offing. The entertainment will also allow me to tick off another good reason for living in this intriguing country.

One of the most rewarding aspects of driving in urban France is the regular opportunity to enjoy street theatre at no more cost than a little time. In towns and cities elsewhere in Europe one is menaced by talentless people pretending to peel an orange, play a saxophone or be trapped behind a glass wall; here the performances are spontaneous and far more entertaining.

Finding myself in a grade II traffic jam on the approach to the town centre, I see that Christmas is quite literally in the air. A yellow lorry is casually blocking the entrance and exit to the car park as a platoon of council workers string up the seasonal lights which will ring the square until the new year is completely bedded in. Sometimes less than a month passes between taking the lights down and putting them up again, although they are officially left in place only until Candlemas in early February. It would obviously be much less bother to leave them where they are all year, but the ceremony and dramas the events offer have become part of local tradition. Technically it is a little early for the decorations to re-appear, but the authorities have obviously chosen today as it is market day and the operation will cause the maximum confusion.

A headcount reveals that the man-to-job ratio is even higher than it would be in Britain. A specialist installer stands on a platform extending from the tail of the lorry, and he has an official with him to ensure he does the job properly. This man is carrying a clipboard and sporting an armband along with his official hat and cigarette, so is probably a Health and Safety Officer checking that the *specialiste* is observing all the regulations for fixing a length of wire to a lamp post.

At ground level are six men in high-visibility jackets and safety helmets with visors and ear-protectors conscientiously in place. As the operation should be comparatively soundless, they may be wearing them on the insistence of the H&S officer, or perhaps to muffle the ribald comments of the healthy crowd of spectators.

The man nearest the tail of the lorry is apparently the mission controller, and is moving his shoulders, raising his arms and leaning over from the waist as if he is assisting the operation on the platform by sheer force of will. His practised movements are quite balletic and rival any mime artist I have seen on the London Underground. Alongside him and spaced out between the tailgate and the lorry cab is the rest of the team. Their individual and joint duties are obviously to offer general encouragement, keep up the cigarette consumption tally and take over shoulder-shrugging and arm-waving duties when the head of ground control grows weary or goes on an official smoke break. The only team member not taking an active part in the operation is the driver of the lorry, who has left his cab with the door open and engine running so that he can have a friendly cigarette and chat with a pair of gendarmes who are clearly on point duty. They have their backs turned to and are completely ignoring the ever-growing queue of motorists, but nobody is complaining. We all know that the job will be done and the blockage removed sooner or later, and any drivers in a hurry now have an excuse and - better still - a bracing challenge to leave their cars in even more awkward locations than that occupied by the yellow lorry.

*   *   *   *   *

In the Bar Fidele I note Madame has joined in the festive spirit, as a single length of tinsel has been strung along the top of Xavier's sole creation. The painting appears to be the right way up today, so the artist has probably been in to redeem, momentarily reclaim and then re-hock his work.

As I order a drink and settle down to wait for Jon, I reflect on the irony that Xavier's painting might one day be judged a modern masterpiece. As Madame observed on my last visit, it looks no better or worse than other daubs which have been enshrined as works of genius. If fate leads that way it will probably be too late for the artist and Madame to profit from any posthumous recognition, but the critics will make a good living from interpreting its significance and value. What they will be unable to explain, however, is why nobody valued it as worth more than a handful of euros during the creator's lifetime.

After irritating the owner by making her bring my drink to the corner furthest from the bar, I see another example of the potential trials and even dangers facing any artist. According to a newspaper on the table, an author in central France is attempting to take a whole village to court for attempted murder.

In his book *Pays Perdu*, Pierre Jourde is said to paint a comic but brutal picture of everyday life in a small hamlet. Written as a novel but based on real characters and events, the depiction so enraged the twenty five residents of the mini-commune that they allegedly ambushed the author on his return to his holiday home shortly after publication of his book. The author claims he was kicked, beaten and even stoned, putting him in mortal fear for his life. In his defence of the non-fiction novel's content, Mr Jourde told the reporter he assumed the stories he relayed were common knowledge, and was shocked to learn that one tale of an adulterous relationship forty years before was unknown to the children of the lovers. According to the descendants, the most worrying aspect of the allegation was that some of them may have married their own brothers and sisters.

I look up and see Madame regarding me with grim satisfaction, then realise that the newspaper may have been deliberately left open at the page featuring the story. The owner of The Bar Fidele will know I am a writer and my stories are based on true events and people. What she will not have considered is that my books are published only in English, and I cannot think of a single French person appearing in them who either reads that language or would be interested in my account of their activities.

Returning to *Paris Soir*, I learn that the mostly friendly invasion of France by Britons is not restricted to those with purely secular interests and lives. France, it seems, is now a leading destination for Christian missionaries from the United Kingdom. It has been revealed in the latest edition of a magazine detailing religious trends that France has overtaken Kenya as the most popular place for Protestant missionaries to answer their calling. Officially, the lack of Protestant churches on this side of the Channel is the reason for the sudden upsurge of interest in a posting to such apparently unenlightened places as Aix-en-Provence or Antibes. I am sure that the missionaries are sincere in their reasons for requesting a transfer, but I somehow fancy that the food, drink, climate and culture in France when compared to the Dark Continent might have something to do with the change in the league table rankings.

*   *   *   *   *

The meeting with Jonathan has sent my black dog loping resentfully away.

After breezing in and ordering a bottle of champagne, my new business partner said that a number of the potential members of our pot commune had contacted him and asked to join the venture; they had also paid a small deposit as evidence of their good intent. Our cartel was now complete, and the commune will be duly notarised tomorrow afternoon. The members will read, approve and sign the individual and mutual contracts and give their cheques to the notaire, then he will formally hand over the keys. Because of the need to re-open our pub before Christmas, the initial and final contracts will be completed on the same day.

But there is even more exciting news from my friend and business partner. The former Entente Cordial is to become the first in a chain of anglo-pubs which will one day stretch from Cherbourg to St Tropez, and perhaps beyond. When I asked him if he had ambitions for world domination by our new style of licensed outlet, Jonathan laughed and reminded me that France also has departments in Corsica and Martinique. He has always liked to think big, he said, and if our initial outlet is as successful as he suspects it will be, there should be no limit to our plans to colonise the rest of the world. As I myself had often said, the Great British Pub is the envy of the world, and there will be no better example than the one we will create in this tiny corner of France.

But, of course, that will take time. From now on, The George will be under my control and I will have my share certificate and managerial status to prove it.

When I asked where and what time the meeting would be, he said that there would be no need for me to attend. The office of the notary dealing with the transfer was on the other side of the peninsula, and as I was not investing financially in the commune, there would be nothing for me to sign. Although I would be responsible for the day-to-day running of the pub, he would apply for and hold the licence. This was not because he did not think I would have any difficulty in winning a licence, but because his notary friend would be able to speed the process up by putting Joanathan's name on the application forms.

My challenge now was to get The George ready for the grand opening. As he reminded me, all the fixtures, fittings and stock were included with the freehold sale of the Entente Cordiale, so we were almost ready for the launch. I would obviously take charge and oversee the cleaning up and re-vamping of the bar to emerge in its new incarnation. His personal view was that we should not try and change too much to begin with. Better to get the bar up and running and taking money, and then we could gradually give the premises the unique atmosphere and character which would become our hallmark.

Tomorrow afternoon Jonathan will be staying on at the office to start the process of applying for the licence transfer and taking care of all the other official requirements of re-registration. As he had said before, the notary is a personal friend of his as well as a business associate, and has more than a little influence with important people in the department. With my agreement he would give the keys to Conan and ask all the members of the pot commune to meet me at The George to start planning the grand opening.

After patting me on the shoulder and raising his glass in salute, he handed me a bulky envelope. When I asked what was in it, he smiled and said it was no more than a small token of his appreciation for helping set up the project. Without me he would have bought another empty and failed bar. Now he and our commune had a stake in an exciting and very rewarding project. The details of my salary and staged payments for my share would be worked out at a later date and at a full meeting of the commune; for now he just wanted me to have a little something to mark the start of our adventure. He added that he knew I am under pressure from the bank and because of what has happened at Le Marais, the contents of the envelope might help relieve a little of that pressure.

*　　　*　　　*　　　*　　　*

I stand outside the Bar Fidele, waving as my friend roars off in his sleek and obviously very expensive sports car. Waiting until he rounds the corner, I tear the top from the envelope and inspect the contents. In these days of credit cards and chequebooks, it is easy to forget what a satisfying feel there is to a thick bundle of banknotes. Riffling through and counting the number of times the number twenty appears, I estimate that there is the equivalent of five hundred pounds in euros in my hand. It is more cash than I have handled for many years, as for some reason my wife believes that I, like the late Queen Mother, have no need to carry money. When I am sent on an errand or go out on my own, she will dole out the basic minimum to cover costs. On the odd times that I do have some money in my pocket it is almost uncanny how this event will coincide with Donella not having her purse to hand when a tradesman arrives for the settling of a bill. Strangely, when I tell this story to most married women, rather than sympathise they tend to smile grimly and nod approval of our arrangement.

But now I have a considerable stash of which my dear wife is unaware, and I will do my best to keep it that way. It is her birthday in two week's time, and this year I will be able to buy her a proper present without having to borrow the money from her to buy it. On our last visit to market I saw her looking wistfully at a top-of-the-range industrial chainsaw. Now it will be hers, and I shall present it on the night of the grand opening of The George Inn.

As I look across the square to see if the owner of the farm machinery stall has managed to breach the barrier created by the council lorry, I see a familiar figure sitting on a moped on the other side of the road. It is Albert Poubelle, and he is obviously watching me. I stuff the money back into the envelope, point at the door of the bar and beckon him to join me for a drink. He shakes his head, raises one arm in salute, then buzzes off towards the market. I acknowledge his wave, and make a mental note to invite him to the gala opening night. I will also ask his cousin, who is the most senior policeman in the area.

If all goes well with our new business venture, I will need to keep on the right side of both these important members of the community. Any local police chief has draconian powers concerning the formal and informal arrangement for the opening times and general running of any bar, and if The George is as successful as I think it will be, Albert's status and influence at the local tip will be of great help when disposing of mountain loads of empty bottles and cartons.

*   *   *   *   *

The sky is still the colour of a prehistoric axe head, but I am in ebullient mood.

My advance from Jonathan Kerr is hidden in the writing shed, and I now have two secrets to keep from my wife. I feel doubly guilty for not telling her about the pot commune and the money, but all will be revealed on the opening night. When she discovers what I have done I think she will be proud of me. It has not been an easy year for us, but things are looking up and if all goes well we should have cause for real celebrations this Christmas. With my income from The George we will be able to re-start work on the conversion of the stable block in the new year, and if our first anglo-pub takes off I will be able to give full reign to my plans for extending the facilities at Le Marais.

With Milly by my side, I am sitting by the duck pond mulling over some new ideas for further facilities at our holiday centre. Donella is in the kitchen preparing a batch of Cornish pasties, rock cakes and a huge tray of bread pudding to sell at the market at Sourciéville next week. I could not tell her that her scheme for raising some desperately-needed cash will become redundant with my income from The George, and she is anyway enjoying the excuse to bake on an industrial scale. I will be happy to eat whatever is left over from the market, though she is confident about the sales potential.

It is true that the French are relaxing their views on what is acceptable to put in their mouths when it comes to food from other cultures, and some traditional British delicacies are becoming almost fashionable. If I make a sign declaring the bread pudding to be a favourite with HRH Prince Charles and made by appointment for him by Donella, I am sure that will help its snob appeal. Despite or because of their egalitarian society, I have always found the French more class-conscious and fascinated by royalty than the average Briton.

This evening my wife will be holding an at-home tasting *soirée* to which she has invited a dozen local expatriates and some of the more broad-minded of our French friends. The party will provide an ideal excuse for me to absent myself and meet the fellow members of the pot commune at The George. I have told Donella that I shall be on the official business of buying drinks for the market organiser at Sourciéville to ensure she is allotted a good pitch. It is yet another lie, but a white one and I am sure she will forgive me when she learns the reason for it.

The watery sun makes a lethargic attempt to put in an appearance, then gives up and retreats behind the clouds. The marshland sits in silence at the bottom of our garden, but I am listening out for any unexpected bellows of pain or screams of terror. It is the time of full moon and Lupin is prowling the marshlands, so I am also keeping an eye on a handful of hardy marsh cattle that are still out to graze. If one suddenly disappears, it will either have found one of the deadly soft spots on the marais or encountered our werecat on a practice run for tonight.

I am distracted by a flash of colour on the far side of the pond, and see that our chickens are also taking the air.

With an almost electric glow to his turquoise plumage, Big Fred is obviously feeling full of himself. Like the head of a middle-class Victorian family on a Sunday promenade, our senior bantam is strutting stiff-neckedly along the bank while nodding haughtily to each side as if greeting imaginary acquaintances and inferiors.

Following in a much more subdued fashion, Barney is affecting a slight limp, and his mood has obviously been as ruffled as his feathers. Behind the two cocks, their spouses Gert and Daisy gossip away happily and I suspect the topic of their conversation will be the latest confrontation between the two roosters. Though one cockerel can meet the conjugal rights of dozens of hens, my wife is a believer in fidelity within any union and insisted that Gert and Daisy should have their own partners. Unfortunately, she has not explained the virtues of monogamy to our birds' satisfaction, and there have been some ugly scenes when Barney has caught his partner *inflagrante* with the real cock of the walk.

As I wag a reproving finger at Fred, Milly sits up, tosses her head coquettishly and begins to preen herself and I realise that another round in the unending game of sexual interplay between the species is about to be played out. I hear a bout of heavy breathing, then the paling fence trembles and groans as a huge head appears above it.

It is the hound of the Basque Quervilles, and Zakur has come to pay court to our pretty collie. The giant Newfoundland lost his heart to Milly when we arrived at Le Marais, and she has enjoyed treating him with disdain. As the great beast slobbers and tries his best to look engaging, Milly finds something interesting at the other end of the pond and prances off with her tail high.

A moment later a much smaller though no less unusual face appears above the fence, and I nod a greeting to Mr Querville. The top of his head is only slightly below that of his dog, so I suspect he is standing on a box. When we have exchanged comments on the weather and disagreed as to the exact hue of the sky, my neighbour asks if it is wise to allow my chickens to range freely on our land. When I reply that the fence dividing our properties seems strong enough to keep them from frightening Zakur, he smiles grimly and says he had heard that the English pride themselves on their sense of humour. But then, he adds, he has also heard that some English people pride themselves on their cooking.

The niceties over, I await the latest doom-laden prediction and am not kept waiting long. Pausing only to arrange his features in an even more mournful disposition, Mr Querville relays today's bad omen. As ever, it concerns the significance of what most people would consider perfectly normal canine behaviour. Last night, says my neighbour in sepulchral tones, one of his dogs began barking uncontrollably. When I respond that that is surely not an unusual occurrence, he says that the dog gave voice exactly on the stroke of midnight. Also, he reminds me, last night was the time of full moon, and a Friday. After I silently make my own prediction of what this disturbing omen portends, my neighbour obliges by informing me that death will shortly be visiting the area. As the local shooting club will be out on the marais in full force for the weekend and the abattoir at Sourciéville is working overtime to cope with Christmas orders, I concede that his prediction may well come to pass. Seeing that I am not taking him seriously, my neighbour gives a theatrical sigh and a knowing nod, then disappears behind the fence.

Whistling for Milly and advising Barney to work on his ring craft before the next bout with Fred, I follow the delicious aroma of baking back to its source.

Although it might appear to an onlooker that Mr

Querville and I do not get on, I think we are both enjoying our daily sessions of verbal sparring. I doubt we will ever be close friends, but we do share more than a fence. As my Basque neighbour says, we may come from very different cultures, but we are both foreigners in a sometimes strange land.

*　　　*　　　*　　　*　　　*

Although the roads in our corner of the Cotentin are quiet at any time, in the small hours they are a desert. Gliding past ghostly hedgerows and alone in my car, I feel cocooned and at peace and safe from whatever the world chooses to throw at me.

French radio can be almost as bad as French television, but I am listening to an interesting programme about one of France's most revered and senior entertainers. Johnny Halliday is the Gallic equivalent of our Tom Jones, but without the looks, original songs or voice. Although older than me, he is a national sex symbol. The most mundane details about his life feature almost daily in some branch of the media, and even the correct spelling of his name is disputed.

Though it has the tone of an obituary, the programme is not being broadcast because Johnny Halliday/Hallyday is dead, but because he has announced his plans to move to Belgium. To many people, this will amount to the same thing.

For some reason, the French choose to view Belgium and Belgians with contempt, and the country and its inhabitants are the butt of countless jokes. I do not know the roots of this malignity, but it is similar to the way we would once delight in mostly unfunny jokes about the Irish. Now that their greatest rock star has declared his intention of becoming a citizen of Belgium, the authorities will probably declare a day of national mourning. To be fair to him, Halliday is half-Belgian, but the French seem to have forgotten that uncomfortable fact.

A fox appears in the headlights, and I see it is

investigating the remains of a creature unlucky enough to have met a vehicle on this lonely lane. I stop and extend an open palm to invite the fox to finish its meal at his leisure, but after looking at me for a moment it slinks off and disappears into the hedgerow. I shrug apologetically and drive on.

I am on the road at this hour because the meeting at the former Good Intent went on much longer than planned. When I return, Donella will hopefully be asleep, and I will not have to tell her more lies about my imaginary meeting with the market boss at Sourciéville.

Our first official meeting was an unexpected success, and it is clear that the members of our pot commune are as excited as me about the prospects for our venture. I arrived to find my fellow entrepreneurs gathered outside the bar, and the normally staid Conan dancing a jig to the bemusement of the old hunting dog. As I drew nearer, I saw he was waving a bunch of keys in the air and holding what looked like an expensive bottle of champagne. When I got out of the car he led the others in a round of applause and invited me to break open the bottle. Then Veronica made a coquettish and very revealing curtsey and pointed to where a pair of bed sheets had been pinned above the door. When I followed her instructions and pulled them aside, I saw that the original sign had been covered with a sheet of lining paper. On it was printed in large letters *The George Inn (Sometimes)*.

After he had explained the joke several times, Conan handed me the keys, took charge of the champagne and invited me to lead the way into our new pub. Savouring the moment, I lifted the flap and walked behind the bar, found some glasses and invited my friends and partners to join me in toasting the success of our joint venture.

For the next hour we drank and talked and wandered around the previously forbidden areas of the premises, playing like children with the light switches and having the first of what will doubtless be many long debates about how the decor, menu and general ambience could and will be improved.

Eventually, we settled down at the bar, and Conan told me about the meeting at the notary's office.

Because of the need to complete the deal before Christmas, the notaire had obligingly agreed to a lunchtime meeting, which showed the esteem in which he must hold Jonathan. Mr Belette had met them at the rear entrance and shown them into the office, and they must have set a record for speed of property exchange. All the papers had been signed and notarised and cheques and share certificates exchanged in less than an hour. The Pot Commune of Nulleplace was now the official owner of the bar, and the notaire had assured its members that Jonathan's liquor licence would be through within the week.

It was now time to get down to the serious business of planning the opening and pre-publicity, and as the only professional in our group I was invited to take the chair. After a short address assuring the commune of my commitment to making The George the most popular and profitable bar in all Cotentin (if not all Lower Normandy), my recommendation was that we should stage an invitation-only celebration the evening before the official re-opening day. This would allow us to entertain the most important members of the community while unveiling our plans for the future of our first anglo-bar.

The event would also allow us to establish and test our systems and services without practising on paying customers. We should not stint on the level and quality of hospitality, and be sure to invite all the most influential and important people in the area. The French members of the community might not be using The George regularly, but it was vital to win their support. We would also need to invite a selection of local settlers to join in the celebrations and hopefully win them as regulars. A poster campaign announcing the official opening day would ensure that every British settler in the area would know about The George and what it offered.

For the next three hours we allotted responsibilities, discussed the guest list, the catering, the dress code and the entertainment for the big night. We argued about the size, colour and wording on the publicity posters, and even the new curtains Veronica insisted we put up before the opening night. But it was a mostly amicable debate. We were all too happy and excited to want to fall out, and as Conan said, although I am the expert at pub-running, it is important that all the members have their say.

Eventually and after yet another toast to the future, we finished our drinks and agreed on the next meeting. After making a final tour of the premises, we turned off the lights, locked the door, then stood outside like regulars loathe to leave their favourite local and start for home.

*　　　*　　　*　　　*　　　*

Pulling into the yard I am surprised to see a light on in the kitchen. Rehearsing my excuses, I walk in to find my wife sitting with our neighbour. Mr Querville is grim-faced and I can see that my wife has been crying. Before I can apologise for worrying her by being so late, Donella says in flat tones that we have been visited by a fox. It came at midnight and got into the hen house. Mr Querville was woken by his dogs barking, and shot it. But it was too late, and Fred and Barney and Gert and Daisy are dead.

After an uncomfortable silence, I walk our neighbour to his gate. When I thank him for his help, Mr Querville shrugs and says it is in everyone's interest to protect our animals from such an evil predator. As usual, the fox did not kill for hunger, but just because it could. He has put the remains of our birds in a sack in the stable block, and did not let Donella see them. When he asks me if I would like the carcass of the fox, I look away and shake my head.

The old man nods and before turning away puts a hand on my shoulder. He says he knows that I am English and have strange ideas about the countryside and nature, but hopes that I have learned a lesson from what has happened. When I say I realise that it seems silly to him that anyone should be so upset by the death of a few chickens, he smiles and says he is not thinking about our birds. It may be unwise to become fond of livestock, but only a real fool invites a fox on to his land.

Nature makes only dumb animals. We owe the fools to society

Honore De Balzac (1799-1850). Journalist and writer, said to be one of the creators of realism in literature

14

The long-threatened snow is with us. The distant rooftops of Sourciéville glitter in a weak winter sun, and our inland sea is a plain of ice. The silence was almost audible as the new day approached, then I remembered that we will never again hear Fred and Barney greet the coming light.

Donella is sleeping, and I will leave her until she is ready to face the day. She was not beside me when I woke during the night, and I found her sitting by the henhouse. When I told her how sorry I was about what had happened, she said that with all the tragedy and unhappiness in the world it was ridiculous to grieve over the death of a few chickens. She is right, but they were our chickens, and I must bear the responsibility for their death.

Because of my stupidity, I now have another secret to keep from my wife. It is not certain that the killer was the fox I befriended, but I cannot help thinking that it followed my trail back to Le Marais. It was only obeying its instinct, and has paid the price and I should have left it to live or die according to the rules and fancies of Nature. Now my sentimentality has caused my wife great sadness.

Mr Querville has offered to pick up some hens and a cock from a farmer friend, but I think it is too soon. Later this morning we will bury the remains in the vegetable patch and there will be more tears, and no doubt our neighbour will see this as another sign of our English eccentricity. It is true that Donella will take comfort in knowing that Fred and Barney and their spouses will be nearby when she is working on her plot, but she will also know that they will help enrich the earth from which she coaxes such an abundant crop.

*   *   *   *   *

Just two days to the grand opening, and I am on a last-minute publicity drive.

After our latest meeting at The George, I had some posters and information leaflets printed and will spend the afternoon distributing them around the catchment area. Due to a language confusion I shall have to dispose of 5,000 leaflets rather than the 500 I thought I had ordered, so have redefined the distribution boundaries.

Donella is selling her pastries and cakes at the Sourciéville market today and refused my offer to help on the stall. This leaves me free to work on the grand opening, but I am running out of excuses for my increasingly frequent absences. My wife is the least possessive person I know and quite happy to be in her own company, but I am sure she knows I am up to something. This morning I deliberately let slip that I am planning a special treat for her birthday, so she will hopefully think I am organising a surprise party.

Another problem is that although I have explained the need for discretion to my fellow shareholders, Veronica insists on telephoning every day to discuss some aspect of how The George will attract customers. I now see it was a mistake to accept her offer to help with publicity and marketing ideas, and she does not seem to share my vision for the sort of entertainment we should offer. I do not think that lap dancing and speed-dating evenings will sit well with the image we want to create, especially as Veronica has offered to be the sole female contributor to both events.

I am also facing budgetary problems even before we are open for business, and have had my first serious disagreement with a shareholder. In his self-appointed role as chairman and only member of the wine and spirits committee, Conan has given me a bill for the vintage champagne he brought to our first meeting. He has also presented me with a long and detailed list of alleged expenses for a weekend visit to one of the most prestigious wine merchants in Paris, and said he had to buy dozens of bottles to sample before placing an order.

His training and past employment as a librarian has obviously predisposed him to having a huge and varied selection of stock for his customers: his situation as a salaried employee of a local authority has also imbued him with a completely cavalier attitude to costs and potential profit margins. When I pointed out that we would have to charge at least ten euros for a single glass from some of the bottles on his proposed list, he said very sniffily that we did not want to attract riff-raff to our establishment.

To prevent that happening, he has also drawn up a list of local expatriates he thinks should be barred from The George before we even open. Looking through it, I saw that the list also includes virtually every member of the French community, including the mayor. When I challenged this xenophobic attitude, he said that he thought the plan was to create the ambience and atmosphere of an English pub and one would not expect to find too many French peasants in any decent local. His attitude is that, in the manner of the best London clubs, we should create an air of exclusivity by being very fussy about who we let through our doors. He also thinks that by keeping prices high and having a strict admission policy, we will ensure that we only attract and cater for the sort of people we would like to rub shoulders with in a favourite pub.

As I responded, if we followed his recommendations there would not be enough customers for him to rub shoulders with; another point for consideration was that he would not be everyone's first choice of a fellow-customer.

*   *   *   *   *

Fifty miles is a long distance to travel to even the most attractive pub, but I have decided to start my poster campaign in Cherbourg.

The main town in the northern Cotentin has more than three hundred bars and restaurants, but with one exception they are all very French.

There is what the owners claim to be an English-style pub near to the ferry port, but the only attempts to capture the ambience of a typical British hostelry are the availability of pint glasses, a very sticky carpet and a selection of what look like punch-holes in the toilet door. The bar is a favourite for British booze-cruisers who come over on the one-day invade-and-pillage package, so I suspect it is they who have made the holes in the toilet door to try to add to the authenticity factor. On my first visit I had to navigate a fight in the doorway and the barmaid tried to short-change me, so the owners are obviously making an effort to make their British customers feel at home. In this instance I agree with Conan about the sort of clientelle we do not wish to attract to The George, so I shall not put up any posters in the vicinity of the Mucky Duck.

Although there is not a large expatriate community in Cherbourg, the ferry port is a funnel for all Britons on route to their homes in the peninsula, so I shall do my best to advertise the attractions of The George in and around this part of the docks. I am wearing overalls and a vaguely official-looking peaked cap, so if I am approached by any

218

representative of the port authority I shall tell them the posters are a ruse to lure the British drivers out of town and on to other less civilized parts of France.

*   *   *   *   *

Arriving at the roundabout on the exit road from the port, I see that a ferry has berthed and is disgorging its cargo. A long line of vehicles leads from the linkspan to the customs barrier, and the British cars are being processed slowly through one channel. The vehicles in the next lane are being waved through without let or hindrance, and this is probably because they have French number plates. In the third lane, the drivers in a static queue of British lorries are being made to pay the price of wanting to bring their goods into another part of the European economic community.

As they clear the barrier, the French drivers hare off like children escaping from school. They are obviously euphoric to be back in their own country, and are already competing to have their first shouting-match or *choc* (their idea of a minor accident) before even reaching the dock gates.

Behind them, the British visitors demonstrate their level of familiarity with driving in France by their approach to leaving the port. The old hands pursue the French contingent as if to show they can drive just as dangerously as the natives, while those for whom it is a new experience wait for a more pedestrian British driver to take responsibility and lead them safely out of town. If the vehicle which takes pole position is not familiar with the rules of the road on this side of the Channel and the driver thinks he is following rather than leading, this tactic can exacerbate the problem. I once saw a lengthy convoy of British cars travelling the wrong way through the roundabout and then down a one-way track into the sewerage plant alongside the main road.

219

But today it seems that none of the more timid British drivers will be led astray, as their progress has been halted by what looks like the daily protest.

In the Fourth Republic, taking to the streets to air a grievance or demand a change has been a tradition since the storming of the Bastille, and is generally regarded as an inalienable right, a duty and a fun day out. Regardless of its outcome, the conduct and highlights of the most minor demonstration are reported in detail in the local press and as eagerly followed by some readers as the sports results. Those taking part vie to be photographed making their heroic stands for liberty, fraternity and usually more pay for less work, and some enthusiasts will travel miles to take part in a march without knowing its ends.

In my years in France I have become caught up in demonstrations against every conceivable issue or perceived injustice. I have even been caught up in protests about the *lack* of protests in support of some unfashionable causes. In general and as with other forms of spectacle, most French drivers are quite happy to be caught up in a *manifestation de solidarité*. It is said that some will actually go out of their way to be held up by a high-profile protest.

Ironically, though nearly all demonstrations are concerned with national or local issues, the most favoured gathering point for demonstrators is at the gates of the port when a ferry is due. British drivers may wonder why they are being made aware of objections to a proposed change to the local canons regarding garbage collection, but the demonstrators know that good timing and location will cause the maximum havoc to traffic and gain the most publicity. Besides, anything that inconveniences English visitors will be generally seen as a good thing.

Leaving my car by the sewerage works and approaching the melee, I see that the cause of the hold-up is a very small affair by local standards. At the entrance to the roundabout, two men are offering leaflets to the drivers of the British cars, and being British, the drivers are winding down their windows obediently and taking them. Nearby, three women are holding up placards, and there is something unmistakably British about the way they are self-consciously muttering rather than shouting their slogans. As I arrive, one of the men hands me a leaflet with a diffident smile; looking at it, I realise that the group is conducting not a protest but an opportunistic sales drive.

One of the placards features a photograph of an imposing town house, another a country cottage. An unusual feature of the cottage is that the bathroom appears to have been installed in the front garden. Below each photograph is a price in euros and sterling.

The leaflet explains that the properties are for sale directly from their owners, and details the accommodations. There is also a long list of all renovation and improvement work carried out, and what each job cost. A quick calculation reveals that the outlay on the town house almost matches the asking price. If the figures with regard to the cottage are accurate, the owners are selling it for less than it has cost them, even had they paid nothing for the building.

Waiting for a lull in the activity, I introduce myself to one of the leafleteers and learn why the group has set up the *alfresco* estate agency. The man explains that he, his wife and her brother and his partner had decided to move to live and work in France last year. They had become involved in a franchise operation selling outdoor hot tubs and spa baths in the North of England, and the sales figures had been disappointing.

The prospects had seemed much brighter in what they thought would be the universally sunnier climes of France, so they had sold their properties in Bradford and relocated the business to the Cherbourg peninsula. Unfortunately, there appeared to be even less call for trendy outdoor bathing facilities in this area, so they had decided to sell up and return to England.

When I ask about the other member of their party, the man says that she is not connected with their business but is

221

the founder of a self-help group they joined recently. The lady with the placard bearing the photograph of the derelict farmhouse lost her job, marriage and all her money after becoming obsessed with restoring a derelict manor house in the Cotentin. Now she runs an organisation for others who have suffered from what she claims should be a medically-recognised addiction, and tries to prevent fellow-sufferers from becoming involved in the cycle of self-abuse. As her leaflet explains, any of the Britons setting out from the ferry port who find themselves overcome with an overpowering urge to buy a ruin in France should immediately phone her hot-line number so she can try and talk them out of it. The service is free, but all users are asked to make a donation to the organisation from the huge savings they will make by using it.

A further incentive is the significant discount to be had on the complete range of hot tubs offered by her new members.

*   *   *   *   *

Sometimes I am privileged to see an example of unassuming fortitude which lifts my soul. The will and spirit to triumph over adversity is what I like most about humanity, and puts our petty troubles in perspective and reminds me of just how lucky I am.

Unfortunately, the feeling does not last, but I suppose that is another human trait, and discontent with what we have is perhaps why we raised ourselves from the primeval sludge.

Earlier today we took tea with an English couple who live in a water-mill not unlike La Puce. We have often driven by and stopped at the gate to look at the pretty little stone cottage and remember what we left behind. This morning an elderly lady was working in the garden and invited us to look round. Like La Puce, there was a small but lively stream winding its way through a water-meadow; unlike La Puce the stream was crystal clear. When I admired how free and clean the water ran, the owner said that she had spent the last year clearing stones from the bed and had used them to make an ornamental rock garden. The garden was at the top of a steep slope and behind the house, and I could not have moved some of the boulders without the help of a mechanical digger or René Ribet's mobylette. When I asked how many men it had taken to do the work, the lady said casually that she had done the job alone. A month before starting the project she had needed a pair of new hips, and wanted to see if they were up to the job. It had been an interesting challenge, she said.

Inside, the cottage was beautifully kept and tastefully decorated except for one wall of the kitchen, which looked as if it had been used as a shopping list for a very myopic person. Seeing my bemused expression, the lady said that her husband suffered from an advanced stage of Alzheimer's Disease. Although lucid most of the time, he would increasingly forget very simple words. When he could not remember the name of a vegetable or piece of fruit, she would write it in large letters on the wall and they would say it together a dozen times. He would forget the words again, she said, but they were there to remind him.

As we looked at the evidence of her husband's crumbling mind, the lady said his illness was particularly ironic as he had been a professor in modern languages. He had been totally fluent in seven tongues, and now could not remember the simplest words of even one. Although it was a bit of a bother to have a basic English lesson at the start of every day, they were both determined to try and halt his decline. As with her rock garden, they both believed in not giving in to age and infirmity. They still had a good life and were happy and much better-off than most people financially, though she would of course give it all away for them to be our age again.

Driving away from the little house, my wife said she would never again laugh at my absent-mindedness, and I promised not to complain about our lack of success with money. I suspect that neither pledge will be kept for long, but I am glad we stopped at the old mill and were reminded of how almost casually cruel life can be.

*   *   *   *   *

Another lesson in natural history and ill-omens from our neighbour.

When we had our daily encounter across the fence, Mr Querville asked if I had heard an owl hooting in the night. When I said this was surely not an unusual or worrying occurrence, he explained that what townies like me thought was a complete owl call was actually an exchange between the male and female. Last night he had heard the 'twit' but not the 'wooh'. This meant that bad luck was on the wing. If I wanted to ensure misfortune did not visit our home, I should nail an owl skull above the threshold. When I said I had seen enough of skulls for the year, he shook his head sadly and reminded me of the recent passing of a widow in Nulleplace. She had heard a solitary owl in the night, and the next day had seen a black cat in her garden. By evening she was dead. When I reminded him that the lady had been over ninety and in poor health, he said that that was just the sort of excuse a doctor would invent. I then pointed out that the black cat belonged to the widow so it was hardly surprising she had seen it in her garden, but he just smiled grimly and said I had a lot to learn about life and death in the countryside.

*   *   *   *   *

The origins of the modern dinner jacket are generally credited to Pierre Lorillard IV, head of a tobacco dynasty which owned land in Tuxedo Park, New York. It is said that Mr Lorillard wanted to rebel against the current cultural standards of Europe, and came up with the idea of cutting the tails from his evening suit before attending a wild ball in 1886.

The inventor of the bow tie is unknown, but I suspect him to have been a descendant of a fatally masochistic member of the Thuggee strangling cult who wanted to know how his victims felt.

Tonight is the big night, and for the grand opening of The George Inn I have managed to squeeze into an old tuxedo lent me by Mr Querville, who predictably claims the inventor to be of Basque origin. He said the jacket was given him by a customer who could not afford to pay his kennel fees, and apart from a number of teeth marks in one arm it is quite presentable. When she handed the coat over the fence, Mrs Querville said that it had been used by her husband to coach a number of their trainee police dogs in riot control, so I should be sure not to be wearing it when I brought it back.

My problem with the bow tie is that Donella is not speaking to me and I do not like to ask her for help in tying it. I spent the last of the money Jonathan gave me on the chainsaw she was regarding wistfully at Sourciéville market, but the gift-wrapped parcel lies unopened on the kitchen table. Although I have told her that we are going out with friends to celebrate her birthday this evening, she is a clever woman and clearly knows there is more to the occasion as I am taking such trouble with my appearance. At worst she knows about my involvement with the re-opening of The George, and at best she may think I am having an affair with voluptuous Veronica.

When returning from yet another late-night meeting of the pot commune last week, I found one of our publicity leaflets on the kitchen table. Beside it was a scrap of paper on which Veronica had written her phone number and address. Being Veronica, she had signed it with a blood-red imprint of her lips. As my wife assaulted an innocent ball of dough, I thought about asking why she had been going through my pockets, then explained that Veronica had given me her number when we had been planning the language courses.

When I asked where she had found the leaflet, Donella said someone put it under the windscreen wiper while she was at the market in Sourciéville. It looked, she added, as if there was at least one other lunatic in the area who thought he could make a go of an English bar and was prepared to throw good money after bad. She just felt sorry for the lunatic's wife. When I said it might be a success if handled properly, she put the dough ball out of its misery with a final *coup de grace* then gave a perfect example of what novelists like to call a hollow laugh.

Later, I heard a noise in the yard, looked out of the window and saw my wife attacking the rose bush by the gate with a pair of secateurs. Although it was dark and snowing quite heavily she seemed to be enjoying cutting the plant down to size, so I left her to it and went to bed alone.

*   *   *   *   *

We are nearing Sousville, and I am about to unveil the reason for my months of duplicity and concealment. My wife is wearing a blindfold, and I took a circuitous route to The George so she would not be able to time the journey and guess where we are going.

Donella is in a better mood now that we are on our way to what she thinks is her special treat, and has brought her birthday present to open at our mystery destination. I am of course concerned that she will not be pleased when I reveal my secret, and have taken the precaution of ensuring there is no petrol in the chainsaw.

We drive into the square, and I am pleased to see that parking places are hard to find. The official start time for the party was an hour ago, and I have delayed our arrival so that we would not walk into a depressingly empty pub.

226

There are dozens of cars lining the normally deserted street, and I see they are mostly British-owned. The majority of our French guests would not dream of arriving on time, and the more important they are the later they will appear. It is quite possible that the mayor will not arrive until the official closing time is past, but any breaches of the licensing laws will not be a problem if they are caused by his late arrival.

Looking round, I see that all seems to have been arranged exactly as planned. On the pavement, Dafyd is in charge of co-ordinating traffic movements and is directing a tractor to the rear of the building. On either side of the entrance, Phil and Phyllis look splendid in identical evening suits, and are taking invitations, handing out carnations and posies while showing guests through the doors. To one side of the entranceway, the massed bands of the Sousville and Nulleplace voluntary fire service are in full dress uniform, and both members are poised to play my wife and me onto the premises. Even our neighbouring dog seems to have entered into the spirit of the occasion, and is enjoying a plate of sausage rolls someone has thoughtfully put out for him.

I turn off the engine and nod to Dafyd, who signals to the band. As they strike up, I help my wife out of the car, wish her the happiest of birthdays and remove her blindfold with a flourish.

*   *   *   *   *

I really think The George will prosper.

I know from experience that any pub opening can be a success if you invite too many guests for comfort and the drinks are free, but seeing the once-empty bar so full has given me confidence. It will also enthuse my fellow shareholders and our guests, and, if all goes well tonight, the costly event will help ensure that we will have plenty of paying customers in the future.

It is a curious aspect of human nature that many people prefer a pub where they have to fight their way to the bar and vie for attention to get a drink. They would also rather beg for a reservation in a fashionable restaurant than go to a less busy establishment where the food is just as good and much cheaper. Success is said to make success, and perhaps they think it will rub off on them. At this early stage, I do not expect every evening at The George to be as busy, but the signs are promising and we have had a very good response from the hundred invitations issued.

At the moment, I am working the room, greeting our guests and generally keeping a low profile. The official arrival time was only an hour ago, and more than half the guests are here. In England they would have been waiting at the doors to claim their free drinks and attack the buffet, but things are done differently here. I have tried to plan and orchestrate the evening as if it were a variety show rather than just the opening of a new bar, and the audience is only just settling down.

Looking around for someone to welcome to our *grand soirée*, I see that Conan is talking at a bemused-looking stranger and seems to be illustrating his remarks by agitating an invisible cocktail shaker with one hand. I join them and learn that the young man has been invited by Veronica, and is a handyman she has engaged to tend to some of her needs in and around the house to which she thinks her husband is not equal. Conan pauses from his hand signals for a moment to explain that Sasha has arrived recently from Brittany and speaks a little English, but cannot understand why the British people he meets seem so amused when he introduces himself. He hands me a card and I see that he is a fully qualified horticulturist, and that his surname is Tosser.

*   *   *   *   *

An hour later and the party is in full swing.

It is a poignant and almost surreal experience for me, as I am surrounded by friends from every stage of our lives in the Cotentin during the past fifteen years. Many of them are regulars in my favourite bars across the region, and there are at least six bar owners who have come along to wish me well.

I said to my wife how touched I was that so many of our landlord friends had taken the trouble to attend the grand opening, but she believes they are hoping The George will fail and I will return to my old drinking haunts. As she says, their businesses must have slumped without my weekly income to rely on.

Although she is clearly not happy about my new business venture, Donella was relieved to hear that I had not borrowed any money to pay for my stake in The George. She now also realises that all the calls from Veronica were about business, so no longer suspects we are having an affair. She was especially pleased to hear that I will be paid for spending most of my time at The George, and we have agreed that my wages will be paid directly into the bank. With the success of her pasty and bread-pudding sales at market, it now looks as if we can survive... and perhaps even prosper.

A whining sound fills the air, and I am relieved to see that its source is not the mournful folk singer from The Flaming Curtains at St Sauveur. Coco the owner promised me that he would confiscate Andre Deprime's guitar before the coach left so we would be spared any traditional airs about disease, death and heartbreak in the Normandy countryside.

The originator of the noise is in fact Kid Nehou, certainly the oldest and probably the most unintelligible disc jockey in the Cotentin, and perhaps even all France. Although his repertoire of record albums is limited to one for each decade of the fifty years he has been a DJ, he is here to organise the karaoke session that is to launch the evening's entertainment. The other committee members were not keen on the idea of inviting guests to show how badly they can sing, but I know they have all been secretly practising their favourite numbers. The added advantage is that I can take over the microphone when we wish to close, and my version of *House of The Rising Sun* will speed the most persistent of guests on their way.

As I clear my throat and thread my way towards the stage to make my first speech of the evening, I see a blue light flashing on the windows on either side of the entrance door. At first I think it is a reflection from the Kid's improvised lighting equipment, then realise the source is outside. Moving to the window, I see that three police cars have pulled up in front of the bar and realise that one of our most important guests has arrived.

Signalling to Conan to begin opening his ultra-expensive champagne bottles, I step outside to find that Albert Poubelle has arrived with his cousin, the local police supremo. There are also at least six gendarmes lining up on the pavement, and it seems they are going to form a guard of honour for their boss.

Adjusting my bow tie, I walk forward to escort our guests on to the premises, but find myself encircled by the posse of policemen. As Albert shakes his head sadly, his cousin curtly informs me that he has not arrived to attend our opening party, but to close the premises and demand that I accompany him to the police station.

As I do my punch-drunk boxer impression for at least the fifth time in as many months, Inspector Dugelle informs me that there are too many charges of illegality to go into at this moment, and he anyway thinks I will not wish them to be detailed in front of my guests.

However, the allegations and resultant charges will more than probably include obtaining money and goods by false pretences, operating a bar without a licence, misrepresentation, gross deceit and malicious trespass.

You can't go home again.

Thomas Wolfe, American novelist

15

Friday, 13th May, 10.30am:

Across the great plain, the creamy hawthorn blossoms signal the approach of what is predicted to be an exceptionally fine summer. The small orchard at Le Marais has been slow to wake, but promises a good crop. It is sad that we will not be here to see the apples grow.

The removals lorry is backed up to the pond, and Stan the Van is persuading a giant gunnera plant to settle between an upturned sofa and Donella's chainsaw and thigh-waders. He will have a more demanding challenge when it is time to load and secrete the barrel of goldfish my wife insists on taking with us. I have warned him about the dangers of close proximity to the descendants of Psycho, and see he has put on a heavy pair of gloves.

Although he has not been in business long, our removal man is an adaptable character and has quickly learned the sometimes unusual requirements and skills involved in moving British settlers. Like so many expatriates we have met in our time in Lower Normandy, Stan has an interesting past and has proved that adaptability is key to success for those settlers who need to earn a living in a foreign land. He first demonstrated he is a natural survivor at a young age, as he has the rare distinction of being a former foster child of the mass murderer Fred West. Also a survivor of several marriages, Stan came to Normandy to start a new life, and has tried his hand at a number of business ventures. He says that helping expats relocate to new homes in other parts of France has proved an interesting experience, especially when the removals need to take place at dead of night.

While I help load the last of our belongings into the lorry, Donella is taking a final look around the house. She will want to leave it spotless, and I think she will also want to be alone as she says goodbye to Le Marais. As she said before visiting her vegetable patch to spend a moment with Fred and Barney and the girls, we have not shared our lives with the old house for long, but it has been an eventful time. As she also said when we walked across the marshlands for the last time, I might not be happy to be going back to England, but at least I will not be spending the next few years in a French prison.

I hear the sound of an approaching Mobylette, and turn to see my friend Albert Poubelle bumping along the track to our gate. He has come to see us off, so is not wearing his official hat. I have left a case of single malt whisky on the table as a farewell gift and acknowledgment of his help during our time here, and have much to thank him for. It is mostly due to his efforts that I am a free man, that the members of our pot commune have got most of their money back, and that Jonathan Kerr and his accomplices are behind bars.

As we now know, the chairman of our association has already spent several years as a guest of the Fourth Republic, and uses a variety of names to ply his trade. According to Albert's cousin, my former friend and partner is not a business consultant or property entrepreneur, but a con man who travels around France taking advantage of particularly gullible Britons. The police chief did not add 'like you' when he said this, but did not need to.

Ironically, it seems there was no carefully organised plan to part the members of the committee from their money. I just seemed too inviting a target when I arrived at The Good Intent. Like a predator sensing an injured quarry, Jonathan had moved in on Simon - and especially Saskia - when he saw the problems they were having with their pub and marriage. When the couple decided to give up on their dream and return to England, he had offered to find them a buyer and they had given him the keys. Because of the legal processes involved, even he would not have been able to sell the bar and pocket the money, but my appearance gave him the idea of making a fairly easy return for relatively little effort. The so-called estate agent Mr Belette was a regular accomplice, and the alleged notaire who took the committee's cheques was another. The notaire's office on the west coast was real enough, which was why Conan and the others had been invited to use the back entrance while Jonathan was buying the real occupier lunch. My part in the proceedings had been to enthuse and enrol the members of the syndicate, and to be left to carry the can when Jonathan and his cronies skipped off to their next arena of operations.

Fortunately for me, Albert Poubelle had reported his suspicions about Jonathan to his cousin at an early stage and been keeping an eye on me and my dealings with him. The trio had been shadowed and picked up on the day of the opening of The George, and before they were able to clear the cheques through a false account. After weighing all the evidence, Albert's cousin decided that I was not a crook, just a fool.

Although perhaps not much wiser after my experiences, I am considerably poorer. Having returned the money Jonathan gave me, we were obliged to pay for the printing of the publicity leaflets, Conan's wine-buying orgy, and the other drinks enjoyed by our guests on the opening night.

There is some good news in that Simon and Saskia have decided to give their marriage and the bar another try. They have also asked if I mind them keeping the new name of the pub, as there has been so much publicity in the region about The George and my involvement that they think the notoriety will be good for business.

Another marginally less dramatic development has been the results of the investigation into the skeleton found in our stable block last year. Exhaustive examination using the latest technological equipment has revealed that the owner was male and probably murdered, but that the crime was committed several thousand years ago. Dating of the bones suggest that the man was a member of an early iron-age settlement, and there is some evidence that he may have been the guest of honour in a sacrificial rite.

The bad news for us is that there has been much excitement in academic circles in the region, and the stable has been designated as a site of special archaeological interest. At this stage there are no plans to do more than continue with the excavations, and my proposal that the regional authorities buy Le Marais and create an iron-age adventure theme park on the site has not been met with enthusiasm.

Whatever happens in the stable block, we will not be allowed to go ahead with the conversion into letting units and our financial situation means we have had to make some very hard decisions.

Without any prospects of income from Le Marais, I am to give up the struggle to make my name as an author. Donella is prepared to carry on, but I feel I have put her through enough hardship and worry. An old friend has offered me the editorship of a catering magazine based in England, and my wife refuses to stay in Normandy without me. I shall probably not find the comparative merits of the various types of deep fat fryers as interesting as writing about our daily lives here, but at least I will be paid for my creative efforts.

So we are leaving Le Marais and Normandy for as long as it takes our financial situation to recover. My friend Albert Poubelle will keep an eye on the big house, and our neighbour has said he will tend our land and look after the wild birds and beasts that have come to depend upon Donella's hospitality.

We have also asked Maitre Lecroix to add Le Marais to his list of properties for sale. Although it is a magnificent house, we both agree that what has happened recently is an indication that we were not meant to settle here.

Our lives were bound to change when we left La Puce, but it seems we took the wrong turning when we came to live in the marshlands. When we sell Le Marais we will be able to pay off our debts to the bank and start more modestly again elsewhere in Normandy, or perhaps in another part of France. It has been a hard choice, but perhaps we have just been going through a bad patch and our luck will change when we move on.

I know many people who have done well with their lives say that the harder they work the better off they become, but I think luck must play a part in all our lives and whether or not we prosper. As my old friend René Ribet says, fortune may be said to favour the bold, but in his experience and observations, it prefers to favour the lucky. Whatever the reasons for our continual money problems, the gods who are said to rule our destinies do not seem to like the idea of our living here, and I think it is time to take the hint.

*   *   *   *   *

The For Sale board is nailed to a sapling Donella planted when we first arrived.

As we enter the tunnel of foliage, my heart lurches as I see that the twee postbox still bears our name as the owners of The Mill of the Flea. For a moment I consider the possibility that our time away from La Puce has been no more than a dream, but reality soon returns.

It is my first visit to our old home since we moved away. Until today, I could not bear to remind myself of what we had left and lost. But now we are going back to live in Britain I feel I must pay my respects to our old friend.

It is no more than eight months since we drove up the track and signed away our home of thirteen years, but seems much longer. I suppose this is partly because so much has happened in our lives since then, but also because of what has been happening to La Puce. The new owners have obviously decided The Mill of the Flea is not for them, and Nature and mischievous human hands have been at play.

The wounded terracotta pheasant still keeps guard atop the ruined chimney, but one of the windows has been smashed and its shutter hangs limply from broken hinges. The drainage pipes I crafted into a fairly effective flue for the wood-burning stove have come away from their brackets, and the pipes lean drunkenly from the gable-end wall.

Crossing the weed-covered terrace, we look through a window at bare boards and barren walls. In spite of its emptiness, the inside of the cottage seems to have shrunk. I see the stain on the floor where a bottle of my nettle champagne exploded, but in the dank and silent interior there are no other echoes of our time here. It is just an empty room in a sadly dilapidated cottage.

At the grotto, the waters of Le Lude still tumble endlessly down to the basin, but the small ponds in the meadow have disappeared beneath a sea of waist-high grass. Beside the Hobbit Tree, one of the hen houses lies on its side, either blown or pushed over. Nearby, the door to the caravan feeding station swings in the breeze.

Sitting on the broken hull of the Water Flea dinghy, I realise why the regular creaking seems unnaturally loud. The surface of the pond lies undisturbed, and the sky above is empty of life. It seems as if it is not only we who have left La Puce. I suspect that the birds and mammals who once made their home here are missing their free board and lodgings more than our company, but it is sad to see they have moved on.

I feel a hand upon my shoulder, and turn to see that

Donella is holding the remnants of a tiny nest. She tells me she found it on the floor of the yard, below the niche where the wren made its home each spring. It looks, she says, as if our little friend has found a better place to live.

It is time for us to go, and as we drive up the track my wife says how poignant it is to see our old home so alone and untended. I nod and mutter my agreement, too ashamed to tell her how I really feel. My heart should be heavy, but it is not, and I think somehow I have been shriven by my return. I would never admit it, even to myself, but I am somehow pleased to find La Puce returning to nature. The cottage and the land and all that happened here were part of us and our life in Normandy. But that was then. We will always have our memories, but the past is past, and The Mill of the Flea lives there.

Epilogue

It seems Normandy is reluctant to let us leave.

The queue of cars waiting to board the ferry has not moved for half an hour, and that is a long time even by French standards. The other lines of traffic are passing steadily through the gates and on to the quay, so I go to investigate.

At the head of the queue, a battered Peugeot with Manche licence plates sits beside the control kiosk, and its driver is enjoying a lively exchange with a ferry company representative. In the car, an elderly lady occupies the front seat, and an even older man sits stiffly in the back. His eyes are closed, and he seems uninterested in the altercation. This is very unusual for a Norman, so I assume he is asleep. I join the driver at the hatchway, and learn that his back-seat passenger will never wake.

The driver, his wife and their uncle are on route to attend a niece's wedding in England. Or were en route. It was not until they arrived at the ferry port that the couple realised their companion had quietly passed away somewhere on the journey from Carentan to Cherbourg.

As the man explains to me, the couple do not intend to take the corpse of their relative to the wedding, and are not expecting to be allowed to board the boat with their passenger. They will take him to the city hospital to complete the formalities, but there is business to do here first. They have paid their fare and are naturally concerned about the rules governing late cancellation of tickets.

To avoid any potential obstacle to a full refund of their money, they have brought the remains of their cousin as incontrovertible evidence of their reasons for not fulfilling their end of the bargain. With an all-purpose shrug, the man says he has already invited the ferry company official to feel for his uncle's pulse or conduct any other tests on the body, so what could be fairer than that?

As the woman in the box reaches for a phone and the driver looks to me for moral support, I smile weakly, offer my condolences and return to report the circumstances to Stan the Van, my wife, dog and cat. When considering some of the situations in which we have found ourselves during our time in this part of France, I do not think that Donella will be surprised to hear the reason for the delay.

*   *   *   *   *

The lights of the town sparkle on a placid sea, and a small fishing smack chugs alongside as the ferry eases its way through the breakwater. Our departure has been delayed by almost an hour because of the incident on the quayside, but the bereaved Norman couple are content as they have been assured of a full refund of their fare.

I wave to the man at the helm of the fishing boat, but he ignores me as he is obviously intent on overtaking us before we reach the open sea. Smoke belches from the wheelhouse as the overworked engine screams in protest, but the ferry is owned and run by a British company so there is clearly a principle at stake. I am reminded of the battle between the tiny car and the giant earthmover in Sourciéville last year, and wave encouragement to the fisherman to show my solidarity. But it is obviously a losing battle, and the man at the wheel throws his arms up in disgust as the ferry picks up speed and leaves his little craft wallowing in its wake. He has failed in his attempt to win this particular race, but I am sure he will be trying again tomorrow.

I hear a grunt of bemusement, and turn from the rail to see a man shaking his head as he watches the fishing boat fall away to our stern. Of about my age when we first arrived in

240

Normandy, he favours a beard, is comfortably overweight and obviously shares my lack of concern for fashionable clothing.

When I ask him the reason for his journey, he tells me that he and his wife have just bought a home in Lower Normandy. The little cottage in the middle of a forest needs a lot of work, but one day and if all goes well they will move over to live in it for the rest of their lives. As he reaches for his wallet of photographs, he tells me they made their decision after reading a book about an English couple who bought an old water-mill in Normandy for next to nothing. Although the writer seemed a pretty hopeless type, the book must have sold millions, and the couple are probably now living happily in a huge *château* in the south of France.

I nod and say I have heard about that book, and it seems to me that life is all about following your ideas and dreams, even if they don't always work out as you had hoped. He agrees and says he has a feeling that, whatever happens to them, his wife and he will not regret taking the big step.

As my new friend invites me to the bar to see some more photographs and hear about their plans for their dream home, I say I will ask my wife to join us and we will be down in a few moments.

He leaves, and I turn back to the rail to raise a hand in farewell to the lights of Cherbourg.

I have no idea what will happen to us in the coming months and years, or how soon it will be before we can return to the country of our hearts. But whatever the fates have in mind for us, I am saying *au revoir* rather than *adieu.*